FAVORITE STORIES OF THE BALLET

For Nadine,
who loves to dance

Text and illustrations copyright © 1984
Robert Mathias, Publishing Workshop

Published in the United States of America
by Rand McNally and Company, 1984

Library of Congress Catalog Card Number: 84-42778
ISBN: 0-528-82178-4

Printed in Italy

Second printing, 1986

FAVORITE STORIES OF THE BALLET

James Riordan

Illustrated by Victor Ambrus

Foreword by
RUDOLF NUREYEV

RAND McNALLY & COMPANY
Chicago · New York · San Francisco

CONTENTS

FOREWORD

FOLKLORE has inspired many masterpieces – in music, just as in art and literature. One has only to think of the many compositions of Tchaikovsky, Rimsky-Korsakov, Stravinsky and Prokofiev that draw on folk music and folk tale themes. Perhaps this reveals the close communion in Russia with nature and the elemental forces of the forest, river and steppe. Who would not be moved by the arrival of the Russian spring after six months of snow and ice? By the boundless steppe and virgin forest stretching endlessly towards the horizon? By the towering pines and firs, the lurking shadows, the menacing wild beasts within the dark woods? Or by a grove of silver birch trees on the banks of a deep blue lake – for all the world like graceful swan maidens dancing?

I have had the good fortune to dance in and to produce all three Tchaikovsky ballets retold here: Swan Lake, Sleeping Beauty and Nutcracker. And I have danced Petrushka. All the tales provide a vast stage on which to express oneself naturally, to breathe freely, to explore all the complex ever-changing patterns of life, to portray the passions of the soul in movement.

It is, if you like, the use of relatively simple means to express great feelings and ideas: the eternal conflict between the powers of good and evil, darkness and light. And no one who tries to create and interpret art can do so in any meaningful way without perceiving and sharing the humanity of its message.

I hope that within this beautiful book, in tale and picture, you too will find artistic satisfaction and accept its invitation to enjoy good music.

Rudolf Nureyev

Petrushka

The story of Petrushka is not based on Russian folk tale, but on the Russian folk theatre. Petrushka is the Russian 'Punch', with a long, hooked nose, wide smiling mouth, two humps upon his back, and a red shirt and cape. Petrushka, (the Russian word for 'parsley') is first mentioned in the Chronicles of the 17th Century as a favourite puppet used by Russian jesters (skomorokhi) at travelling fairs.

When the Russian composer Igor Stravinsky came to compose a ballet based on the puppet Petrushka, he worked with his friend, the Russian artist Alexandre Benois, to write a libretto based on traditional Russian puppet shows.

The ballet was first shown in Paris at the Théâtre du Châtelet on June 13, 1911; it was performed by the Ballets Russes, with the famous dancer Vaslav Nijinsky as the tragic Petrushka, Tamara Karsavina as the flirtatious ballerina whom he loves and Orlov as the Mighty Moor.

The final act of the ballet is set in the great square of Saint Petersburg at a winter fair. Originally, the choreographer, Mikhail Fokine, had over a hundred people in this crowded scene and, for the first time in ballet, used only natural movements to create realistic crowd scenes.

Igor Stravinsky

PETRUSHKA

FAR away across the Russian steppe there lived a little boy. It was his birthday, and his Grannie gave him a rag doll she had made out of coloured bits of cloth.

Misha was delighted with his present. 'I'll call him Petrushka,' he said, hugging the rag doll tightly.

'Who's he calling names?' the rag doll wondered. 'Could it be me?' It was indeed, as the doll soon realised. 'Well, that's as good a name as any, I suppose,' he thought happily.

Just then Grannie murmured half to herself, 'Do you know, I pricked my finger sewing that doll. That means he'll have bad luck, poor little fellow.'

She looked at Petrushka so sadly that he could not help smiling back at her, in the hope of making her feel more cheerful.

'He's got such a funny smile though,' she continued, 'I expect he'll survive somehow.'

As Misha ran to kiss his Grannie, he slipped and upset a bucket, dropping Petrushka on the floor. The doll was swept along on a rolling wave of water right up to the stove.

'There, what did I tell you!' said Grannie laughing. 'He's in trouble already but there's no real harm done.'

As Misha helped to mop up the water, the rag doll sat drying by the stove.

It was a happy house and Petrushka loved to listen to the fairy tales Grannie told to Misha every evening and the soft low folk songs she sang as she worked. Petrushka especially liked the smell of her pies baking on fresh spring mornings, when to be hungry was a pleasure. But the dark winter

Petrushka listened too, until his tired little eyes could not keep open

evenings were the best of all, when husky bearded men and plump, pink women would crowd into the cottage out of the snow to sing and dance to the music of a mouth organ or an accordion. Sometimes, when they were tired, they would just sit round the table, listening to Grannie's stories. Petrushka listened too, until his tired little eyes could not keep open any longer.

Up in the loft of the wooden cottage lived five kittens: four females and a tom called Alexander. Misha had found them abandoned in the street and brought them home. He and Petrushka would take them fresh milk and scraps to eat each day, and play with them in the bales of hay.

One day, however, all their happy games came to an end: Misha had to go away to school in the city of Saint Petersburg. Petrushka was left behind, forgotten.

Time passed and still Misha did not return. The four female kittens grew up and ran away; no one came to feed them any more. Only the tabby Alexander remained. The house was quiet and lonely now. Grannie went about very sadly, growing thinner every day and often gazing dimly into space, as if preparing to fly away.

One day she was gone.

In her place came a stranger with a black bushy beard. He brought with him a chill, unfriendly feeling that had never entered the cosy home before.

'This cottage is mine now,' he said, shooing Alexander out and tossing Petrushka into an old oak chest.

That night Petrushka made up his mind to run away. 'Grannie's gone,' he sighed. 'Misha's far away at school, and now Alexander's disappeared. What am I to do?'

Then he had an idea. 'I know, I'll make my way to Saint Petersburg to find Misha.'

When it was dark, Petrushka climbed out of the chest, left the cottage and hurried through the village. But which way was the great city?

He had not gone far when he heard the cheery sound of sleigh bells and soon a white horse came in sight, pulling an old man huddled in a big fur coat.

'Hey, stop, stop,' yelled Petrushka. 'Are you going to Saint Petersburg?'

But the fur-clad figure did not see him through the whirling snowflakes, nor hear him above the noise of the horse's thudding hoofs. The white horse heard him though, and slowed down to a trot.

'Do you want a ride with us, Rag Doll?' he asked.

'Yes please,' Petrushka cried, nodding his head eagerly. 'I want to go to Saint Petersburg.'

He climbed into the sleigh behind the dozing man and snuggled down into a sack of sunflower seeds. The sleigh bumped on across the snow-white plain and through a fir-tree wood. Petrushka fell into a happy sleep.

When he awoke he found himself in the corner of a cottage room; the

white horse, the fur-clad driver and the tinkling sleigh had gone. Now he heard merry voices, caught the heady smell of fresh-hewn wood, and saw a jolly fellow approaching.

'Hey, Katya, come here quickly,' said the man. 'Here's a new playmate for you. Goodness knows what he's doing in this sack.'

That was how Petrushka came to live with the carpenter and his daughter Katya. The days flew by contentedly, the weeks turned into months, and then to years. Katya grew up and no longer played with her rag doll. Instead she went for walks with boys and gazed from the window dreamily. Once again Petrushka was lonely and neglected; he longed for company.

One day a poor washerwoman came to the carpenter's cottage, with four ragged children trailing behind. How the poor children's faces lit up when they saw the funny doll.

'Wouldn't it be fun to live with those children,' thought Petrushka.

At that moment, the youngest child picked him up, then, as his mother called, just as abruptly dropped him on a blob of glue left on the carpenter's workbench.

'Here's my chance,' Petrushka thought.

In an instant he had hopped into the woman's bag and, since the seat of

Petrushka would yell from
behind the stove, 'Pay up at once'

his pants was covered in glue, he stuck to the bottom of it. Without noticing, the woman carried him home along with her washing.

So began a new life for the little doll. He helped the poor washerwoman as she went about her work and, if a mean client refused to pay, Petrushka would yell from behind the stove, 'Pay up at once or I'll turn your house into a pigsty!'

Thinking a hobgoblin was watching, the frightened customer would at once fuss about the washerwoman, giving her the money owing to her, and sweets and cakes into the bargain for the children.

Petrushka would chuckle with delight.

A day came, however, when the poor washerwoman had to wrap up all her belongings in a shawl to take them to market. She needed money to buy food for her starving children. So Petrushka found himself upon a stall amid old straw hats, an odd shoe and glove, rusty nails and hooks, tattered books and cracked plates, an old mug and a broken clock. Late that afternoon, Petrushka heard a voice so rough it made him tremble.

'I'll take that rag doll,' it said, 'and make a puppet out of him.'

Two copper coins were tossed into the bowl and Petrushka was snatched up by one of his legs and carried off upside down.

'You're going to be a clown in my theatre,' said the man. 'When people see your rags and silly face – those big saucy eyes and cherry-red nose – they'll split their sides laughing.'

Shortly after, the rag doll was thrown into a wooden box; the lid was slammed shut and he was left in darkness. This was to be his home, and prison, for a long time to come.

Petrushka became a clown in the puppet show. At each performance he was punched, tripped up, knocked about and laughed at constantly. And straight after every show he was flung back into the box and taken off with the other puppets to the next village fair.

At last the puppet show came to the city of Saint Petersburg. By now, however, poor Petrushka had forgotten why he wanted to visit the great city. Even if he had recalled the wooden cottage and Misha who had gone away to school, it would have been no good: for the boy was now a man.

Petrushka was excited by the dazzling city all the same, by the cries of little children, the bustling crowds, the colour and the noise. Whenever daylight rushed into the dark world of his box, he would leap out, turn head over heels and land right on the stage. The children shrieked with glee;

Petrushka very soon became their favourite puppet.

He visited Saint Petersburg many times after that; and always at Easter or Christmastide. The puppet master would put up his stage amid the performing bears, the gaily-coloured swings and the noisy crowds, and for the carnival he would put on a special show, featuring the Mighty Moor, Koshchay the Skeleton, Golubushka the Ballerina and, of course, Petrushka the Clown.

Koshchay the skeleton was a mean and miserable puppet. He liked to think everyone was afraid of him; so Petrushka would tremble and shake whenever he approached and make out he was scared. That pleased the Skeleton so much his old dry bones would rattle gleefully.

Golubushka, on the other hand, was very beautiful and Petrushka grew to love the pretty ballerina. When she made an entrance in her lavender dress, she would twirl round and round the adoring rag doll, shake her golden tresses in his face and trip lightly away, as if he was not there. It was always the same: he adoring, she disdainful of his love.

After one performance, Petrushka found a tiny velvet flower at his feet; no doubt Golubushka had dropped it while dancing. He picked it up, gazing at it lovingly, his tiny heart fluttering like a butterfly.

So happy was he that he began to dance upon the darkened stage. Such a sad, tender, beautiful dance. If only an audience had been there to see him glide and leap so gracefully about the stage. No longer would they have seen the jerky steps and tumbling falls of a clown.

But no one saw him. No one knew.

Next day was a holiday, the highlight of the Christmas carnival. Amid the throng, pushing past the stalls of toys, coloured balloons and gingerbread, past the groups of whirling Cossacks, raucous Gypsy singers and a military band, was a young nursemaid with her charge, a child wrapped up like a ball of fur. If you took a closer look you might just see a tiny button nose and the wide eyes of a little boy. His eyes gleamed from all the exciting sights and sounds.

'I want to see Petrushka,' he exclaimed, pulling his nursemaid's hand.

'Of course,' she replied. 'How can we come to the fair without seeing him?'

Her cheeks rosy with the frost, the nursemaid pushed her way through the crowd to the very front and stood before the stage.

'Roll up, roll up, Ladies and Gentlemen!' the puppet master was shouting. 'Come and see the Mighty Moor thrill you with his strength and skill.'

The scarlet curtains of the small theatre parted to reveal an oasis of palm trees amid scorching yellow sands; by the trees stood the giant figure of the Moor, a bejewelled turban on his head, a curved sword at his belt. Gleaming white teeth flashed and sparkled beneath a flowing black moustache as he picked up a sack of coconuts and slowly raised it three times above his head, his brawny muscles rippling with the strain.

The children and their nursemaids gasped in admiration.

Thereupon, the pretty Golubushka made her entry, wearing a gold taffeta skirt. The soldiers whistled, the nursemaids blushed, the children stared wide-eyed. As the scenery changed from scorching desert to a snow-swept Russian plain another figure took the stage: this funny fellow took two faltering steps, fell flat on his face, looked and waggled his red nose.

How the children laughed, crying out, 'Petrushka, dear Petrushka!'

While the puppet master was urging on the children to poke fun at the Clown, the Mighty Moor swept Golubushka off her feet in a wild dance around the stumbling rag doll.

'Look at the silly Clown! See the Moor carry off the pretty Ballerina!' shouted the puppet master.

That was the cue for Petrushka to start his clumsy dance. Yet today he felt a strange sensation in his heart: love pangs for Golubushka and jealousy for the Moor. Why did he always have to be the Clown and not the Ballerina's partner?

He sat there gazing at Golubushka as if in a trance, his legs unwilling to obey his head.

'Come on, Petrushka, make us laugh,' the children cried impatiently. Still he did not move.

Abruptly, the scene came to an end, as the puppet master brought the curtain down. Then, grabbing Petrushka by the scruff of the neck, he threw him hard into the box, slamming down the lid.

Petrushka sighed, two lines of tears trickling down his cheeks. 'Oh Golubushka,' he murmured sadly. 'If only I was as mighty as the Moor, I could save you from him and the cruel puppet master. I would take you in my arms and carry you to the tallest tower in Saint Petersburg: I'd lift you high above the city. People would stare up and say: that isn't the sun shining, it is the lovely, radiant Golubushka.'

Then, with a sob, he reflected, 'But I'm not strong and I'm not big; I'm just a nobody.'

Overcome by tiredness, he floated gently into a dream. And in his dream Golubushka was at his side, confessing that she loved him really. Though she danced with the Moor, her thoughts were always with the little rag doll. Giving him a kiss, she slowly faded from his dream and he woke up in the darkness of his box.

Meanwhile, the Ballerina was on stage, twirling round and round. 'Surely there is no one in the whole world as beautiful as me,' was her only thought. 'No one has skin so pale and fine. Such deep blue eyes, such dainty feet.'

So proud was she that she leapt higher and higher to show off her good looks and flirt before the Mighty Moor. As the crowd applauded admiringly, she thought to herself, 'How everybody loves me.'

The Moor caught her round the waist and whisked her off in a passionate dance.

'If only Petrushka were here to see them dancing . . .' said a small child in the crowd.

Golubushka heard him, paused and wondered, 'It would make him so unhappy he would cry. He is always kind to me; no one else is kind. Not that mean old puppet master, nor the selfish Moor, nor the Skeleton who hates everyone: Petrushka is even kind to him; and when I'm with Petrushka I don't feel scared at all. Petrushka loves me truly, that I know.'

But then all thought of Petrushka vanished as the Moor swept her up once more into another frenzied dance.

'Come on, Petrushka, make us laugh'

At the side of the stage stood a figure watching. It was Petrushka, pale and determined. With an enormous effort he had pushed open the lid of his box and now stood staring at the scene. His mind was set: he would challenge the Moor to a duel and show Golubushka how brave he was. Even if he were slain, it would be no worse than forever being mocked and knocked about.

Suddenly he heard the clank, clank, clank of bones creeping up behind him, and there stood the Skeleton with his white toothy grin.

'Just look at them,' Koshchay said in a hollow voice. 'See how close they hold each other; see how fondly Golubushka gazes into the Moor's dark eyes. Why don't you challenge him to a duel?'

Blind with jealousy, Petrushka rushed on to the stage and threw himself upon the Mighty Moor. His puny firsts hammered on the chest of the astonished giant.

'You think you can treat Golubushka as you wish,' he cried, 'just because you're big and strong. And you think I'm nothing but a silly clown with no heart at all. Well, you're wrong. I do have a heart and I have feelings.'

Slowly the Moor understood, he rolled his great dark eyes in rage, puffed out his enormous chest and drew his sharp curved sword.

The crowd held its breath. Golubushka threw herself between the two, but was knocked aside by the angry Moor.

'Run away, Petrushka,' she shouted. 'He'll kill you for sure!'

At the edge of the stage Koshchay, chuckling to himself, hopped up and down, his bones clicking and clacking all the while.

The puppet master looked on amazed. But he did not step in. 'Why worry?' he said to himself with a grin. 'This unexpected show is pulling in the crowd.'

By now the Moor was bearing down on poor Petrushka, waving his sword above the rag doll's head.

'Run, run, Petrushka,' cried the children anxiously.

But the soldiers and the nursemaids jeered at the little doll, certain this was all part of the fun. When Petrushka tried to climb down the steps at the front of the stage, they pushed him back again. His escape at the back was blocked by Koshchay and the puppet master.

He was trapped. With a roar of triumph, the Moor thrust his sword deep into Petrushka's heart.

The pretty Ballerina screamed and fell down in a faint beside the lifeless body.

Poor Petrushka. In the moment of his death, scenes from the past flashed vividly before him: he saw the faces of all the people who were dear to him. How often he'd thought of them and now they were all here with him.

'Here's Misha,' he wanted to cry out. 'He's found me, after all. We had such happy times together, didn't we? And there's Grannie, dear kind Grannie, who told such wonderful fairy stories. She didn't die, after all. Here comes my tabby friend Alexander swishing his long tail; so he's followed me all the way to Saint Petersburg. And the old white horse, I know you: you gave me a ride in the sleigh. Katya, Katya, are you here too? And your father, the kind carpenter. You, too, poor washerwoman: how are your children now?'

With a happy smile, Petrushka closed his eyes and felt himself rising up as on a cloud and floating, floating a long, long way away.

'Get up, Petrushka, make us laugh,' shouted the children urgently.

He did not stir.

'It's only make-believe, isn't it?' asked an uncertain voice.

As the rag doll still did not move, a cry went up.

'He *is* dead! The Moor has killed Petrushka.'

An icy blast of wind blew through the fair. The soldiers and the nursemaids shivered, the children wept bitter tears. Why had it turned so cold all of a sudden? The nursemaid with her little furry bundle turned to go. Her eyes, like those of the little boy, filled with tears.

Seeing the commotion, a policeman came towards the stage.

'Now then, what's going on here?' he asked gruffly.

'Nothing, nothing at all,' the puppet master hastily replied. 'It's a lot of fuss over nothing; this rag doll here needs throwing out. He's come to pieces, that's all.'

The policeman shrugged his shoulders and, like the crowd, drifted away to other stalls. Had he turned back he would have seen Koshchay the Skeleton grinning and rubbing his bony hands.

'Here I am. Here I am'

Yet then, all of a sudden, a shrill voice rang out from above the roof of the theatre.

'Here I am. Here I am.'

Everyone looked up. And people cried, 'Look, there he is. It's Petrushka. He didn't die, after all. Hooray for Petrushka.'

The puppet master's mouth gaped open. Looking down aghast at the broken rag doll in his hand, then up at Petrushka, alive and laughing on the roof, he fell down dead from shock. The Skeleton, his grin faded to a scowl, shuffled off into the night. The pretty Ballerina smiled fondly through her tears. The children cheered and waved their hands.

Flying above the fair, Petrushka danced happily in the frosty evening sky as he'd never danced before. Kind, brave Petrushka would live forever in the hearts of children everywhere.

Swan Lake

This popular German theme provided the basis for Peter Tchaikovsky's first ballet, commissioned by the Russian Imperial Theatre. The composer began work in August 1875 and finished it in April 1876. Before its premiere, he was asked by the Ballerina P.M. Karpakova to insert a Russian dance for her in Act 3; he did so and the ballet was first performed on February 20, 1877 in Moscow's Bolshoi Theatre, with Reuzinger as choreographer and Ryabov as conductor. Karpakova danced the dual roles of Odette and Odile.

It had a mixed reception. The Russian Theatrical Gazette described the sets as drab, the performance as mediocre, the conducting unimaginative and the music monotonous and boring. Not an auspicious start for what is now the world's most popular ballet!

It was to be thirteen years before Tchaikovsky wrote another ballet. Today it is hard to realise just what he had achieved with Swan Lake. For the first time he had given ballet dignity, elegance and genuine feeling. He created great dancing as well as great music, combining the grandness of a symphony with the colour and artistry of dance. This had never been tried before.

Swan Lake was not seen in its present form until 1895, when Tchaikovsky was already in his grave. The ballet was subsequently given a new ending for the Bolshoi Theatre in which good triumphs over evil, although the Marinsky (now the Kirov Theatre in Leningrad) retains the original version, in which the two lovers jump into the lake together and drown.

The final scene in which Prince Siegfried fights the wicked wizard now provides one of the most dramatic dances in the entire ballet.

Peter Tchaikovsky

*At dawn next day, Prince
Siegfried rode out of the palace*

SWAN LAKE

ONCE upon a time there lived a widowed queen who had only one child – a son. Though he would soon be twenty-one, to his mother's sadness, he was still unwed; Prince Siegfried much preferred hunting in the forest to a quiet life at home.

But now that he had come of age, his mother pressed him to choose a bride and have children who would one day rule the realm.

'I do not wish to take a wife, dear Mother,' he replied to her entreaties. 'I wish only to be free.'

When his mother grew cross with him, he sighed, saying, 'But there is no one that I love.'

To celebrate his birthday, the queen arranged a palace ball, to which she invited daughters from the richest families in the land, and princesses from over the sea.

Before the ball, she told Prince Siegfried sternly, 'Now, my son, you will choose your bride from among the noble ladies at the ball. That is my command.'

Prince Siegfried bowed in resignation.

'Very well, Mother, be it as you will.'

The queen hoped that when he saw the fine beauties at the ball, there would surely be one to take his fancy. However, because she loved him dearly, she also said, 'Tomorrow, go and enjoy yourself with your companions at the hunt. Perhaps the sport will help you to forget your cares.'

At dawn next day, Prince Siegfried rode out of the palace with his band of friends. But although they galloped wildly across the plain and through the verdant forest, and soon had a goodly bag of game, the prince was still unhappy. A dark cloud of gloom hung above his brow: he had no eye for the beauty all about him, no ear for the birdsong, no heart for the chase.

As twilight fell and the hunting party turned for home, they found themselves in the shadow of a dark, still wood, where no bird sang. Just as they were riding by they heard a whirring overhead. When they glanced up, they beheld a flock of wild swans, their long necks outstretched flying through the evening sky.

The prince startled his companions with a cry, 'Look, do you not see the leading swan? It bears a golden crown.'

His friends murmured in surprise: for no one saw a golden crown, however much they strained their eyes.

'It must be the Swan Queen,' exclaimed the prince excitedly, his gloom now scattered to the winds.

He had once heard tell of a queen of all the swans who might be seen in the evening sky. By now the wild swans were almost out of sight, lost above the gaunt, still trees of the enchanted wood.

The prince at once set off in pursuit, plunging through the trees.

The hunters stood in eerie silence for a moment. Then, following the prince, they dismounted, turned aside from the path and made their way into the dark, primeval wood. The gnarled oaks and elms towered high above them like guardians set to bar the way. The damp moss underfoot muffled each wary step; the vine and bramble tripped them up. Soon they were lost in a dark green world of ghostly shadows. Gladly would the men have turned for home. How would they find the swans in this dense maze?

But Prince Siegfried's heart was gripped by some strange longing. He pressed on and on until, all of a sudden, a gleam of silver light appeared between the trees, and the band emerged on the banks of a broad lake, glistening in the moonlight.

There, far out in the centre of the lake, swam the flock of snow-white swans, their graceful figures gliding on the rippling water. How lovely they appeared! Yet how sad and lonely they seemed in the twilight.

Prince Siegfried raised his bow, took aim at the Swan Queen, then, with trembling hands, lowered it again.

'To shoot that swan would be like killing love itself,' he said. 'She is like a noble maiden, so proud, serene and fair. How I would cherish her as my wife.'

There swam the flock of snow-white swans

The prince's companions were shocked. A prince marry a swan? Had the wood bewitched him? To them she was but a bird, swimming on the lake; an easy target for their bows.

Then it was too late to aim: startled by the shadows on the shore, the swans were stretching out their slender necks and spreading their broad wings. In a moment, their arched bodies took wing together, leaving scudding silhouettes on the surface of the water. Their shadows swept across the faces of the watching men.

Before his comrades could restrain him, the prince had dashed off in pursuit once more and was soon enveloped in the forest gloom. When the huntsmen did take up the chase, they found their feet entangled in the undergrowth and their path blocked by a wall of trees.

'The prince has lost his mind,' one grumbled.

'He'll lose his way and dear life too,' another said.

But the prince was running fast and true along a path that opened up before him and drew him on towards the flying swans. It was not long before he emerged into a clearing; how surprised he was to see ahead the black broken rocks of a ruined castle, its single tower looming like a giant fist threatening the sky.

Ahead were the black broken rocks of a ruined castle

Swan Lake

Being weary, the prince sat down upon a rock to rest.

'How shall I find my Swan Queen in this godforsaken place?' he sighed.

Yet as he gazed into the gathering gloom, he saw a figure shrouded in white mist gliding towards him. And as the moonbeams illuminated her, he saw a mortal maid, her long fair hair blowing in the breeze. A billowing white gown concealed her slender form as she walked towards him on bare feet.

The prince only knew the vision to be real when it addressed him in a human voice.

'Prince Siegfried, you should not have come. An evil sorcerer lurks hereabout; he will do you harm.'

'But who are you?' asked the prince. 'Can you truly be the swan that bore the golden crown?'

'It is I,' the maiden sighed. 'I am the daughter of a far-off king who roused a wicked wizard's wrath. That evil monster, lord of this enchanted wood, cast a spell on me and on my handmaidens: he turned us into swans.'

'If you are a swan,' exclaimed the prince, 'why do I see you now as an earthly maid?'

'Each night, as darkness comes, we take human form,' the princess explained. 'And then at dawn our pale arms sprout white wings once more, our necks grow long and our backs are covered with swansdown. As for me, since I am the daughter of a king, my hair turns to a heavy crown of gold.' She gave a sobbing sigh.

After a while she began again. 'The sorcerer is cruel. He mocks and taunts us: if you listen closely you will hear his scornful hissing through the leafy summer trees, his crackling laughter in the winter frosts.'

The prince's heart was pierced with pity for the poor swan maid. He took her pale hands in his, saying boldly, 'I shall save you, dear Swan Princess; I would give my life for you. Such love has never entered my heart before. Tell me, pray, your name.'

The princess blushed and lowered her lovely head. 'I am Odette,' she said.

There was an awkward hush between them. Then the maid spoke up again. 'When you gazed at me from the lakeside, it was as though your eyes caressed me. How I longed for you to follow. So I flew slowly to guide your way. No mortal has ever seen me take my human form. Only you, dear Prince.'

'Then I shall never let you go,' he cried. 'You will remain with me, Princess, one day to be my queen.'

'No, no, dear Prince,' cried Odette, tears welling in her eyes. 'At dawn's first light I must become a swan again and fly away.'

'Is there nothing I can do to release you from the spell?' the prince asked in desperation. 'Surely there is some way to overcome the wizard's power?'

The swan maid was silent. Then, at last, she murmured shyly, 'There is one way. But it is hardly possible. A man must be found to give a promise of everlasting love. That would break the spell, and I and my companions would be free.'

'But I love you dearly,' said the prince. 'I'll always love you and never betray you for another. You are saved, dearest Odette.'

'We shall see how lasting is your love,' she sighed. And her deep blue eyes, that had just now shone with hope, clouded from uncertain fear.

The prince would gladly have taken her in his arms to reassure her, but at that moment she was gone, vanished in a wraith of silver mist, melted into a cluster of glistening moonbeams.

Prince Siegfried searched about him and called into the night: he told her of the coming ball, begged her to come to the palace, so that he might announce her as his bride. That would break the spell. But his voice echoed back unanswered from the broken rocks, and his only reply was an owl hooting mockingly from the castle ruins. He was alone once more in the cheerless glade.

Just then, guided by his shouts, the prince's companions appeared out of the trees. Together they made their way back through the silent enchanted wood to where they had left their horses, and they set off for home.

As they rode along, the prince was very quiet, lost in thought; now and again he glanced up to the sky. Was it the fleeting moon or did he really see the shadow of the lovely swan princess, flying through the sky, wearing her golden crown?

Next day, the palace was bustling with arrangements for the ball. The cooks and kitchen-maids prepared a sumptuous meal, the grooms and gardeners cleaned and tidied the stables and the lawns; the chambermaids and footmen rushed up and down the staircases, dusting, bowing, polishing and curtseying and adding to the general din.

Amid the bustle, the Lord Chamberlain strode importantly about the ballroom directing operations, and cuffing the pages' ears when they got in his way. Meanwhile, in red cap with tinkling bells, the court jester darted to and fro, poking fun at the pompous lords and ladies, especially My Lord Chamberlain himself.

Towards evening the guests began to arrive, some from lands beyond the seas. As they paraded through the palace halls, the great crystal chandeliers overhead flashed and gleamed, reflecting the precious jewels and medals that adorned their rich clothes.

All the eligible princesses from far and near had been primped and powdered, bustled and bound, coached and corseted, each hoping to be selected as Prince Siegfried's bride. The mothers sat proudly by their daughters, fanning themselves in nervous expectation. Fathers twirled their long moustaches, calming nerves with a glass of this or that.

Little did anyone divine that the prince had already made his choice, and was even now anxiously awaiting the arrival of his dear Odette that he might announce her as his bride.

At a signal, fanfares rang out, the tall gilt doors at one end of the ballroom opened, and in came the royal train with the queen leaning on the prince's arm. The royal pair moved sedately past the guests, towards the two thrones on a dais at the far end of the hall. When they were seated, the musicians in the minstrel's gallery struck up a waltz and the royal ball got under way.

'What exquisitely beautiful maids,' the queen whispered to her son. 'And all of them daughters of counts and kings, rich barons and well-to-do boyars. Surely you can find a worthy bride amongst them?'

Her clothes matched her companion's, being deepest black

The prince kept silent.

His mood was not for dancing. Even the exciting czardas left him unmoved; he watched unsmiling as the foreign princesses danced before him in the gay Spanish fandango, followed by the colourful Neapolitan gavotte, then the whirling Russian gopak and the stately Polish mazurka. As each dance ended, it was applauded warmly, while Siegfried sat as in a dream, glancing constantly towards the doors.

All of a sudden, trumpets rang out as two unexpected guests appeared, a tall red-bearded nobleman clad in black and, on his arm, a strikingly handsome princess, dressed severely in a long gown. Her clothes matched her companion's, being deepest black.

She was the living likeness of the swan maid.

Truth to tell, the girl was none other than Odile, daughter of the evil sorcerer on whose arm she leaned. Her father had turned her into the image of Odette, so that the prince might be deceived and break his pledge.

The herald announced the new arrivals: 'Baron Rotbart and his daughter, the Princess Odile.'

As the pair approached the queen, Prince Siegfried gripped the arms of his throne in great excitement: surely this princess was his dear Odette? She looked just like her. And yet there was something sinister in her eyes. But no, it had to be his fancy. This was Odette, whom he had invited to the ball!

He rose to take her hand and, leading her to the dance-floor, he danced with her as if he'd never let her go.

'Odette,' he murmured tenderly, 'I thought you would never come.'

She looked up at him and smiled. As they danced the wizard's daughter, as cunning as her father, held Siegfried's eyes captive with her own, preventing him from looking towards the window behind the throne. For suddenly a white swan had appeared, beating its wings against the window pane.

The white swan was, of course, Odette, to whom the prince had pledged everlasting love. Since it was not yet time for her to take her human form, she could only gaze in from outside, trying to warn him.

All evening Prince Siegfried danced with the enchanting Odile, unaware of the deceit. Although his heart felt pangs of doubt at first, the longer he held the black-clad maiden in his arms, the more he was bewitched. And when the last waltz brought the birthday revels to a close, Prince Siegfried took the false princess by the hand and led her to the smiling queen.

'Your Majesty,' he announced, 'I have chosen my intended bride.'

As the queen gladly nodded her assent, the evil Baron Rotbart stepped between them to take his daughter's arm. In a rasping voice, he addressed the prince. 'Will you swear to love none other?'

The prince looked surprised, still blind to the unhappy swan beyond the window. Now it beat its wings even harder in one final effort to warn him.

In vain. The prince was too much in love to notice.

'Upon my heart, I swear to love this maid as long as I shall live,' he solemnly declared.

No sooner had he spoken than there came a crash of thunder, the chandeliers grew dim and an icy wind swept through the room. In the darkness mocking laughter echoed around the walls, and an eerie greenish glare revealed the evil wizard and his daughter, laughing at the prince. Before anyone could move, they had fled into the night.

Only then did the prince realise what he had done: Odile was not Odette!

There came a crash of thunder and an icy wind swept through the room

The evil pair had made him break his vow to the lovely swan maid. Now she was doomed for ever . . .

But then, in the flickering candlelight, there came excited shouts, 'Look, look. There, outside the window!'

As all faces turned, they saw a white swan with a golden crown hovering at the window, flapping its heavy wings, straining its graceful neck. In an instant it had vanished in the gloom.

'Odette,' cried the prince. 'How could I deceive you! Please, oh please, forgive me.'

Before anyone could stop him, he rushed headlong from the palace in pursuit of the fleeing swan.

Coming to the enchanted wood, the prince ran blindly through the trees until he arrived at the forest lake. But no swan ruffled its moonlit calm, no form cast a shadow on its silvery bowl.

Quickly he dashed farther to the glade, and there beheld first one, then two and more maidens dancing in the moonlight. Soon a whole troupe of dancing maids, dressed all in white, appeared, each stepping lightly behind the other, gliding mournfully across the grass.

It was the swan girls, released, deep in the night, from their enchantment.

How beautiful they were. Yet none could compare with the lovely Odette, the swan maid whom he loved. But where was she now?

His heart beating wildly, he watched spellbound from behind a tree, hoping to see his own true love. Finally, he could bear the pain no longer and dashed out towards the group: the startled swan girls barred his way, as if protecting someone. He rushed to and fro between the maidens, searching desperately for Odette.

Then at last he found her, standing all alone, her fair head bent in sorrow, her slender limbs quivering beneath her thin white gown. As he went to take her in his arms, she moved away, seeking protection with her maids. The prince would not be denied; he dashed after her, finally catching her in his arms, and he lifted her lovely face to his.

Her tearful, accusing glance pierced his grieving heart.

'Can you not forgive me?' he begged. 'I did not mean to betray you. I was blinded by my love.'

'But she had a different name,' Odette said reproachfully.

'I was confused,' the prince replied. 'Her name was so like yours.'

'Yet not the same.'

Prince Siegfried buried his head in trembling hands. There was such anguish in his shaking form that pity touched the swan maid's heart and she relented.

Putting her hands gently on his shoulders, she murmured, 'I forgive you. But now it is too late. Nothing can save us from our fate.'

Thereupon the lovely swan maid ran from him. Her heart, so filled with

*The strength ebbed
from her limbs*

love, now burst with pain and sorrow; she no longer had the will to live. All the colour drained from her face, the strength ebbed from her limbs. Her swan-like arms quivered and rose as she feebly hovered twixt life and death. The dying swan girl sank slowly to the ground, surrounded by her handmaidens. She lay there still and white upon the grass.

'Odette, you must not die! My love is pure and true,' the prince shouted so loudly it made the black rocks of the ruined castle tremble. 'I shall break this accursed spell!'

Just then, the evil sorcerer flew down into the clearing in the shape of a giant owl. He had come to mock at Prince Siegfried's grief.

'So you thought you could save your love and defeat my mighty power!' the great bird hissed, its eyes glinting in triumph! 'Now she is dead, you cannot have her.'

In a fury, the prince threw himself upon the sorcerer and there began a

struggle to the death. The mortal prince was no match for the wizard, who soon had his claws about the young man's throat. Yet somehow love had given Siegfried superhuman strength, and he broke free.

Before the frightened swan girls, the two foes fought across the glade; several times the giant owl threw Siegfried upon the ground and seized his throat, it seemed the prince's strength was waning and he would soon be overcome.

Yet again and again he fought back, determined to avenge his true love's death. Finally, with one last effort, the prince tore off one great owl's wing, and the sorcerer, with half his power destroyed, fell stricken to the ground, his single wing flapping grotesquely in the air.

Seizing his chance, Prince Siegfried leapt upon his foe and quickly tore off the other wing, so draining the wizard of all his power.

The wretched wingless body now writhed in its death throes across the ground and finally came to rest, still and dead as stone.

The prince had won.

Yet in his victory, he had also lost. For Odette lay motionless amid her maids. Kneeling by her side, the prince gently pressed a kiss upon her death-cold lips.

As he did so, a warm and gentle breeze sprang up, the trees about the glade waved their branches and, with a terrible crack and roar, the black-stone castle ruins crumbled into dust.

Siegfried stared at the stricken maid. A tender blush spread across her cheeks, her eyes opened as if from a long, deep sleep, and she smiled.

'My dearest Prince,' she whispered, 'you have brought me back to life and saved us from the evil spell.'

All around them life was stirring in the early morning light; the happy, smiling maidens embraced their freed princess, overjoyed to retain their human form with the coming of the dawn.

As the happy group made its way through the wood, they caught the sound of distant calls and horns, and soon came upon a palace party of riders despatched to find the prince.

What a joyful reunion then took place. The glad tidings were sent ahead to the anxious queen and quickly spread throughout the land. Prince Siegfried soon wed his dear Odette and all the world rejoiced with the happy pair.

The power of Love had overcome the force of Evil.

Cinderella

Perhaps the best-known fairy story in the world, it was published by Charles Perrault in his Histoire ou Contes du temps passé *in Paris in 1697, and set to music by several composers. Marius Petipa used the story for Baron Schell's music, the ballet being performed in Saint Petersburg in 1893. And it was used by Fokine to the music of D'Erlanger for the Ballets Russes in 1938.*

But the most enduring Cinderella ballet is that by the Russian composer Sergei Prokofiev, Zolushka *(Cinderella). With choreography by Rostislav Zakharov, it was first performed in Moscow's Bolshoi Theatre on November 21, 1945, just two months after the end of World War II.*

Cinderella was danced by Olga Lepeshinskaya, the Prince by Mikhail Gabovich; a little later the ballerina Galina Ulanova made the role of Cinderella famous all over the world. The first British version, staged at Covent Garden on December 23, 1948 by Frederick Ashton, used many traditional ideas from the British pantomime, particularly the amusing Ugly Sisters (played by Ashton and Robert Helpmann); Moira Shearer danced Cinderella and Michael Somes the Prince.

Sergei Prokofiev

CINDERELLA

THERE was once a wealthy gentleman who lived happily with his wife and daughter. His wife was the kindest person in the world, and the little girl resembled her mother in every way, being modest, gentle and good-natured. But the good wife died and the gentleman remarried, this time to a widow who had two daughters exactly like herself: stuck-up, vain and disagreeable.

No sooner was the wedding over than the stepmother began to ill-treat her husband's girl. She was so jealous of the child whose goodness showed up the horrid nature of her own two daughters that she gave her all the rough work to do about the house. The poor girl had to scrub the floors, wash the dishes, dust the stairs, make the beds, even rake out the cinders of last night's fire and light another at dawn. She was on the go from morn till night.

Her bedroom was in the cold, dark attic, where she slept on an old lumpy mattress. Her stepsisters had rooms with shiny wooden floors, four-poster beds and mirrors in which they admired themselves from top to toe.

Yet she suffered all in silence, not daring to tell her father lest he should suffer on her behalf: for his wife was in charge about the house.

Of an evening, when her work was done, she would sit in the chimney corner of the kitchen, close to the warm ash and cinders of the fire. Because of this the elder sister called her Cinders, though the younger softened it to Cinderella. Yet even in her ragged clothes she was still a hundred times prettier than her sisters – and them in all their frills as well.

One day, the king's son held a ball to which he invited all the high society of the town. Of course the two vain sisters were on the guest list since they

*Yet she suffered
all in silence*

were members of the fashionable set. How proud they were. For weeks before they talked of nothing else:

'What party dress am I to wear? Red velvet plush with English lace?'

'Oh dear, I'll have to lose a pound or two.'

'Shall I have my hair in ringlets or set back, bouffant style?'

'What's in fashion now – high heels or low?'

Poor Cinderella was kept very busy ironing underclothes, starching petticoats, sewing, washing and darning. She even had to give advice on what looked best – since she had better taste than her two stepsisters. She helped them look as pretty as she could; she curled and crimped their hair, dabbed rouge and powder on their cheeks, pulled their corsets tight.

Do you think they were grateful? Not a bit. As she did their hair, they poked fun at her:

'I bet you wish you were going, Cinderella.'

'What a laugh: Cinders at a ball! What would the prince say?'

'Would you wear your sooty frock or the one with patches?'

How the sisters laughed.

Any other girl would have refused to help them but Cinderella smiled good-naturedly and did her best.

On the day of the ball the two sisters did not eat a thing; they spent hours and hours before the mirror, trying to look just right; more than a dozen laces snapped as they squeezed their stomachs into corsets which were much too small in an attempt to give themselves slender waists.

At long last it was time to leave. Off they went in their carriage to the royal ball. Cinderella watched them sadly out of sight, and sat on her little chimney stool and cried.

Suddenly, wonder of wonders, her Fairy Godmother appeared. 'What's the matter, child?' she said.

'I wanted so much . . . to go . . . to . . .' But her sobs choked her words.

'You wanted to go to the ball, is that it?'

Cinderella nodded her downcast head.

'Well now,' said the Fairy, 'if I arrange it, will you promise to be a good girl always?'

Cinderella nodded once again.

'Then run into the garden and fetch the largest pumpkin you can find.'

She did as she was bid, bringing the finest, ripest, roundest, orange pumpkin she could find. But, she wondered, how could a pumpkin help take her to the ball?

Scooping out the inside of the pumpkin, the Fairy then tapped the shell with her magic wand. Instantly it became a golden coach.

'Now fetch the mouse cage from the pantry. Let's see if we've trapped some mice.'

There were six mice scrambling about inside the cage. As Cinderella opened the mouse-trap door, the Fairy tapped each mouse gently on the head as it ran out. In an instant each mouse became a splendid horse. So the coach had a team of six mouse-coloured greys: all they now needed was a driver.

'Shall I see if the rat trap has a rat?' Cinderella asked. 'We could make a coachman of him.'

'Good idea,' said the Fairy. 'Go and see.'

Of the three fat rats within the trap, the Fairy chose the longest whiskered one. With a tap of her magic wand she made him into a fat jolly coachman, clothed in velveteen with great bushy whiskers.

The Fairy Godmother smiled at Cinderella. 'Go into the garden, dear, and bring six lizards from behind the water barrel.'

These were turned into tall, slim footmen in gorgeous green tunics, who took their places upon the coach, three before and three behind. You would think they had been born to the job!

'There now, my dear, you have a coach, six dappled greys, a driver and twice three footmen. They will take you to the ball. Are you happy now?'

'Oh yes,' said Cinderella. 'But do you think I should go in this shabby dress?'

The Fairy smiled. Touching Cinderella with the magic wand, she turned rags to riches in a trice. What a lovely sight! Her grimy tattered frock became a gown of silk and lace, embroidered with silver and gold, and sparkling with precious gems. Her long hair shone like burnished sunshine and on her dainty feet were the prettiest glass slippers ever seen.

'Off you go, my dear. But remember one thing well: be home before the clock strikes twelve, not a minute on. The magic only lasts that long. At midnight the coach becomes a pumpkin, the horses mice, the driver a rat, the footmen lizards and your riches rags.'

Cinderella agreed to this condition and went off joyfully to the ball.

When informed that an unknown princess had arrived, the prince himself bustled out to greet her. He led her on his arm into the ballroom past the assembled guests.

Silence. Not a word. The dancing stopped, the music ceased, all stood staring at the lovely sight. Then a buzz and hubbub filled the hall.

'I say, how splendid. How absolutely marvellous. Who can she be?'

A gown of silk and lace, embroidered with silver and gold

The ladies looked hard at every detail of her hair and clothes; on the morrow they would copy the fashion she had set – as long as such splendid cloth, and craftsmen to fashion it, could be found.

Even the old king's eyes popped out as he stared in admiration, remarking to the queen that he had not set eyes on such a pretty thing in donkey's years.

'Not since you were young, at any rate, my dear,' he added hastily under the queen's stern look.

Meanwhile the prince had led Cinderella to the place of honour and sat her down, then shortly requested the pleasure of a dance.

She danced. Oh how she danced! So gracefully that she was even more admired. She and the prince whirled about the ballroom to the strains of violins – and gasps of wonder from the crowd. Then the banquet began. But not a morsel passed the prince's lips: he had lost his appetite and all the while gazed fondly at Cinderella as she moved among the guests and finally sat beside her sisters. She asked politely how they liked the ball, offered them oranges given her by the prince, and generally made them feel at home.

Of course, they never dreamed that the beautiful princess was Cinders.

In the middle of their talk, she heard the palace clock strike fifteen minutes to midnight. Straightaway, she rose, curtseyed to the crowd and left as quickly as she could. When she was home, a minute before time, she found her Fairy Godmother waiting for her news.

'Please may I go to the ball again tomorrow: the prince has decided to hold a second ball and I am invited!' These were Cinderella's first words once she had finished thanking the Fairy again and again for her kindness.

While she was busy telling about the ball, Cinderella's stepsisters knocked loudly at the door. The Fairy Godmother vanished and Cinderella went to open it.

'You're very late,' she said, yawning and rubbing her eyes, as if to remove the sleepy dust.

In truth, sleep could not be further from her mind.

'If you had been at the ball,' said one sister with a sneer, 'you would not yawn your head off, Cinderella. The most beautiful princess in the world was there.'

'And if you want to know,' the other said, 'she sat next to us and shared her presents with us.'

Cinderella pretended not to care but asked the name of the fair princess.

'Nobody knows,' they said together.

'The prince was ever so upset when she ran off. I'll wager he'd give the world to know her name.'

At that Cinderella sighed and gave a wistful smile.

'How lucky you both are. If only I could see her.'

Next evening the two sisters went off to the second ball and were followed a little later by Cinderella, even more radiant than the night before.

The prince just would not leave her side; he danced with no one else and confessed how much he loved her. Cinderella was so happy that time

slipped by unnoticed and she forgot her godmother's words. Only when the palace chimes fell on her ears did she recall:

One, two, three . . . 'It must surely be eleven.'

But, no, it struck twelve times!

Midnight!

Cinderella leapt up and fled as swiftly as a deer. Although the prince sprang up in pursuit he could not catch her; all he found was one glass slipper upon the palace steps. Lovingly he held it in his hands.

The guards were questioned: had they seen a lady pass?

No, no one had seen a beautiful princess, only a shabby serving wench in a ragged dress.

Cinderella arrived home quite out of breath, having run all the way. Nothing remained of her coach or footmen, her finery or jolly driver. They had all vanished like a puff of smoke. All but the two glass slippers: one with the prince and one upon her foot.

When her stepsisters came home, Cinderella asked about the ball. Was the princess there once more?

Eagerly they told her all they knew: how the princess had fled at twelve o'clock, and in such haste that she had lost a slipper. All that Cinderella knew. But then they recounted how the prince sat sadly in his chair, gazing fondly at the slipper of glass, and thinking only of his lost princess.

He was plainly head over heels in love.

And that was true. For a few days later, a proclamation came:

Hear Ye! Hear Ye!
His Royal Highness Will Wed
The Maid Whose Foot Fits This Slipper

And the little glass slipper was paraded through the town on a velvet tray.

First, all the princesses from miles around tried it on, then duchesses and ladies of the court. All in vain. Finally it was brought to each house in turn and at last it came to Cinderella's home. The stepsisters had a go: they squeezed and pushed, but their feet were much too big.

Cinderella watched. She knew it was her slipper and murmured, 'May I try? Let me see if it will fit my foot.'

Her sisters burst out laughing. But the man whose job it was to find the owner of the slipper was willing to let anyone try. He looked closely at the girl and saw how pretty she truly was.

'My orders are not to miss any maiden,' he said. 'Sit down, young miss, and hold out your foot.'

The little slipper slid on easily, as if made for her alone.

You could have knocked the sisters over with a feather. Their faces dropped still more when Cinderella pulled out the matching slipper and put that on as well.

Just at that moment, the Fairy Godmother appeared and, with a touch of her magic wand, changed Cinderella's rags to riches as before. Thereupon even her sisters recognised the fair princess of the palace ball.

They fell on their knees to beg forgiveness for all the unkind words and deeds they'd said and done. But kindly Cinderella raised them up and kissed them.

'With all my heart I forgive you,' she said. 'Let us love one another from now on.'

Without more ado she was taken to the prince and he married her the next day. And since she was as good as she was beautiful, she brought her sisters to live with her at the palace; within a time they learned to be more loving, and so found good husbands in their turn.

Giselle

The story of Giselle was written by the famous French poet Théophile Gautier together with the Marquis de Saint-Georges: it was based on a poem by the celebrated German writer Heinrich Heine. The Frenchman wrote the story for the Italian ballerina Carlotta Grisi to perform in a ballet for which the French composer Adolphe Adam wrote the music.

It was first produced at the Paris Opera House on June 28, 1841 by the French ballet masters Jules Perrot and Jean Coralli. Lucien Petipa (brother of Marius) danced Albrecht and Carlotta Grisi – Giselle.

Giselle is a role that virtually all the great ballerinas have wanted to perform – Anna Pavlova, Tamara Karsavina, Galina Ulanova and Margot Fonteyn. Among the most famous Albrechts have been Nijinsky, Rudolph Nureyev and Anton Dolin.

Adam was the first composer to use leit-motifs – short phrases of music which are repeated whenever a particular character appears. These phrases are heard whenever Giselle enters and are accompanied by certain dance steps, but not always the same ones: they vary as she changes from a simple village girl to a mad creature and then to a wistful, loving spirit.

The story's ending has varied over the years. In the original version Albrecht was reconciled with Bathilde at the wish of the dying Giselle. In later versions, Bathilde does not reappear and Albrecht either falls dead as Giselle vanishes from sight, or falls sobbing on her grave as the curtain falls.

Giselle, performed at the Paris Opera House in the 19th century

GISELLE

IN the dark forests of Silesia dwell the Wilis, the ghostly spirits of maidens who have died in grief before their wedding bells could chime. They have died not by natural means, but of broken hearts after being jilted by their lovers.

These poor maidens are unable to rest peacefully in their damp earth graves. For they all have a burning passion to dance; their feet itch and tap and cannot keep still. So at midnight they rise up from their earthy beds and gather in bands upon the forest paths, there to seek partners for their dance.

Attired in their white wedding dresses, whose hems are ever damp, with crowns of lilies on their heads and shining gold rings upon their fingers, the Wilis dance in the moonlight like fairies. They laugh with such easy joy, they beckon you on so enticingly with welcoming arms, their faces are so sweetly innocent that no one can ever resist their invitation to dance.

It is no wonder, therefore, that young men do not dare venture after midnight into forest glades where the Wilis are thought to dwell. Even young women are often warned by parents to avoid such places, especially if they are very fond of dancing. Indeed, girls with a passion for dancing, it is thought, are more likely to become Wilis should they die young and broken-hearted.

One maid whose mother was always scolding her for dancing was Giselle.

'You are too fond of dancing, my girl; one day you'll pay for it with your life. Just mark my words!' Giselle's mother warned.

But Giselle paid no heed. She danced and danced to her heart's content, just when and where the fancy took her. So lovely was she that all the

village youths would try to dance with her; yet none could match her nimble feet.

One day, as Giselle was dancing with her friends, a royal hunting party passing through the forest stopped for refreshment in the village. The hunters mingled with the throng watching the whirling dancers. So enchanted was one man with Giselle that his heart pounded in his breast and, afterwards, he could not chase her from his thoughts.

He was Albrecht, the handsome young Duke of Silesia whose castle lay on the mountain slopes overlooking the village.

'My father would not let me marry a village girl,' he reflected gloomily. 'And she would never consider me as a friend, as I am – with my fine clothes and servants.'

But there was a further thought: Albrecht was already engaged to a wealthy countess, and blue blood always mixes with blue blood, even in fairy tales. After all, the royal marriage would bring him more land and wealth. Would he give up all that for this dancing village maid?

So fierce was Albrecht's passion, however, that his heart now ruled his head. 'What if I dress in simple village clothes and say I'm from across the

As Giselle danced, a royal hunting party
stopped for refreshment in the village

mountain? No one will know me and I may win the maiden's love.'

Thus with the aid of his young squire Wilfred, he took to visiting the village, staying in an empty cottage across the way from the home where Giselle lived with her mother Berthe. He would arrive in stealth, cast off his rich cloak, plumed hat and sword, and put on peasant garb. Thus disguised he would mingle with the villagers, introducing himself as Loys, a simple village lad.

It was not long before he made the acquaintance of Giselle, and charmed her with his witty tongue and noble looks; innocently, she took him for what he said he was. They met several times, their fondness growing with each meeting. How happy Giselle was to see him dance, for he danced with more grace and passion than other village lads – even Hilarion, her most devoted boyfriend.

Poor Hilarion was bitterly jealous. He loved Giselle deeply and resented the handsome newcomer. His dark suspicions grew and grew: he wondered who Loys really was and why he had appeared so unexpectedly. And there was something about his rival that reminded him of a person in the recent past . . . Deeply mistrustful, Hilarion decided to keep a close watch on the man who had stolen his sweetheart's love.

One morning early, Hilarion was standing uncertainly before the door of Giselle's cottage; he had come in one last attempt to win back her love. Nervously he was about to knock when he heard the sound of approaching footsteps. In haste, he dodged out of sight behind the cottage fence and waited for the intruders to pass.

As he peered out from his hiding place, he saw two men approach and stop outside the cottage opposite. It was Albecht, Duke of Silesia, and his squire Wilfred, deep in conversation and unaware of the prying eyes. Uneasy at his master's adventure with the village girl, Wilfred was trying to dissuade him from continuing with his plan. But Albrecht refused to listen to advice and angrily handed him his cloak and sword, bidding him place them in the cottage and return to the castle forthwith. Full of foreboding, Wilfred was obliged to obey.

In the meantime, Albrecht, now disguised as Loys, boldly walked over to Giselle's door and knocked loudly. Just to tease her, he hid from view amidst the trees as she ran out eagerly to greet him. And then began a happy game of hide-and-seek, with Albrecht teasingly blowing kisses to show her where he was before darting behind another tree or shrub. At last she caught him and, tired from their game, they sat down together upon a

Albrecht refused to listen

'Beware, Giselle, your lover
is false and will betray you'

wooden bench and rested in the early morning sunshine.

Albrecht quickly stole a kiss and pledged eternal love, 'Giselle, you are the only girl I've ever loved; I swear I'll be true to you forever.'

Shyly Giselle picked a daisy at her feet, then tore off the petals one by one, nodding and shaking her head in turn.

'He loves me, he loves me not,
He loves me, he loves me not . . .'
And so on until just one petal remained.
'. . . he loves me not.'

Sadly she flung down the flower and began to cry. But Albrecht quickly plucked another daisy and picked off its petals, making sure he ended with, '. . . he loves me.'

That soothed her qualms and together the two danced in each other's arms in the glade between the cottages.

It was then that Hilarion chose his moment to intervene. Torn by jealousy, he could restrain himself no longer and rushed from his hiding place to stand, arms folded, before the startled pair.

'You should be ashamed of yourselves, kissing and cuddling in full view!'

Furious, Giselle sprang up and scolded him, 'And you, why do you spy on us? Go away and leave us in peace.'

Stung by her harsh words, Hilarion fell to his knees and tried to put into words the feelings in his heart. Surely his own deep and long-suffered love was more valuable than this stranger's passing whim?

But Giselle only laughed and mocked him, turning her back.

Deeply hurt by her taunts, he then blurted out what he had seen, warning, 'Beware, Giselle, your lover is false and will betray you!'

Thereupon, Albrecht quickly jumped up and attacked the jealous man, driving him with his fists into the forest. When Hilarion had fled, the peasant-duke returned to his beloved just as a lively group of village girls and boys arrived carrying baskets of grapes.

It was the grape-harvest season, and all the young people were gathering to pick the fruit of the vines and celebrate their work in festival. Putting down their baskets, they now began a merry dance which Giselle eagerly joined, whirling round and round, her feet hardly touching the ground. The young people sang and danced and laughed, and made so much noise it disturbed Giselle's mother.

Throwing open her cottage door, Berthe shouted just one word, 'Giselle!'

Smiling, the boys and girls circled round her so that Giselle could hide behind their backs. But Berthe soon pushed them aside and dragged her daughter from their midst.

'Stop this dancing at once,' she cried. 'One of these days you'll dance yourself to death, my girl!'

Scolding her daughter for wasting so much time, Berthe took her roughly by the arm and pushed her inside the house; but not before she shook her fist one last time at Albrecht.

A gloomy hush now descended on the merry group, scared in spite of

themselves at the mother's warning. The lads and lasses went off to the fields in silence to resume their grape-picking.

Albrecht was about to return to his own cottage when he heard a sound that made his heart jump to his throat. A distant hunting horn! Afraid that the royal huntsmen might uncover his secret if they found him in his peasant clothes, he hastened after the others towards the vineyards.

He was just in time, for the hunting party was arriving at the village. It was led by none other than the Prince of Courland with his daughter the Countess Bathilde – that very girl to whom Albrecht was engaged. They had journeyed to Albrecht's castle and, not finding him at home, had spent the day in sport, escorted by Albrecht's squire Wilfred. Now, tired and thirsty, they stopped to rest at Giselle's home and take refreshment.

Flattered at the visit of such noble guests, Giselle's mother curtseyed before the party and at once had a table and chairs brought out and set down

before them. Giselle then brought a pitcher of wine and goblets for the royal guests.

While they were drinking, Giselle edged timidly towards Bathilde to admire her fine silken riding dress; kneeling down she put the train to her cheek to feel the fur-edged hem.

Unaware that this simple maid was her rival for the affections of the Duke, Bathilde was touched by her action. She patted Giselle's head and bade her rise.

'My dear, what do you do here in the village all day long?' she asked.

'I sit and spin,' Giselle replied.

'And is that, dear girl, your heart's delight?'

'Oh no,' Giselle said. 'Most of all, I love to dance.'

And before anyone could stop her, Giselle whirled about in a dance that made the head spin, ending flushed and glowing with a curtsey to her ladyship.

In the background, Giselle's mother hissed her disapproval.

'That girl will dance herself into an early grave! She'll become a Wili, sure enough.'

Yet the Lady Bathilde was entranced and, wishing to comfort the girl who was upset by her mother's words, asked her more questions about herself. When she learned that Giselle had a handsome sweetheart, she threw up her hands in joy, exclaiming, 'Well, how delightful. I too am a bride-to-be, my dear. My sweetheart is a handsome duke.'

Then taking off her own pearl necklace, Bathilde slipped it over Giselle's pretty head, so that it lay gleaming about her neck.

At once Giselle kissed the lady's hand in gratitude, before running to her mother proudly to display the royal gift. The young maid was quite overcome with joy and could hardly thank the countess enough before her mother ushered the guests into the cottage to rest.

Before entering, the Prince of Courland instructed Wilfred to sound the hunting horn should he be needed. But as soon as the prince and his daughter had disappeared into Berthe's home, Wilfred hung up the horn by the cottage door and went in search of Albrecht.

Some time later, the village boys and girls returned gaily from the fields with the peasant-duke in their midst. Seeing no sign of the royal visitors he naturally assumed they had left. While he busily chatted to the lads, Giselle was being hoisted on to a table outside her cottage door and crowned with vine leaves as Queen of the Grape Harvest. When he saw her, Albrecht ran

*'My dear, what do you do
here all day long?'*

to take her in his arms and twirl her round the glade in a happy dance.

It was then that fate intervened.

For the jealous Hilarion had stolen into Albrecht's cottage and found his fine cloak and sword. Triumphant, he rushed forth and thrust the two lovers apart; holding up the noble cloak and glittering sword, he shouted

for all to hear, 'There, I told you so! This man is false. He is no peasant as he claims.'

In the silence that ensued, all eyes turned to Albrecht. But Giselle thrust Hilarion aside and, going up to Albrecht and putting her arm on his, gently asked, 'Is it true, my love? Is this sword truly yours?'

For a moment Albrecht hung his head, cheeks flushed, then all of a sudden he snatched up the sword and dashed at Hilarion, intending to run him through. But his way was blocked by other youths, giving Hilarion time to run to the cottage door, seize the hunting horn and blow a loud blast upon it: once, twice, three times.

In a trice, the Prince of Courland emerged, followed by Bathilde and her ladies-in-waiting. Of course, they recognised Albrecht straightaway, and were astonished to see him in peasant clothes.

'What is the meaning of this?' exclaimed the Prince.

'Why are you dressed this way, my beloved?' asked Bathilde. And she went up to Albrecht and kissed his cheek in greeting.

Dropping to one knee, he kissed her hand, then hung his head in silence.

Giselle, meanwhile, was watching all with mounting anxiety; suddenly, she forced herself between the countess and the duke, and confronted Albrecht.

'Who is this woman, Loys?'

Albrecht stayed silent.

Turning to Bathilde, Giselle asked, 'Are you his bride-to-be?'

Frantically signalling to the countess to keep silent, Albrecht was nonetheless too late; Bathilde nodded her assent.

In a frenzy, Giselle tore off the necklace and flung it to the ground; then running to her mother she threw herself face downwards at her feet, sobbing as if her heart would break. The remorseful Albrecht rushed to her side, trying to calm her, while her friends all crowded round in pity.

But she would not be comforted. After a while, she rose unsteadily to her feet and wandered about apparently mad with grief. Her gaze was wild, her long dark hair unloosed, and she ran to and fro as if she no longer saw anything or anyone around her.

Then, in an instant, her eyes lit up and she fell to her knees before a cluster of daisies, as if recalling the dawn of her love. Plucking an imaginary flower, she began to tear off petals, murmuring all the while,

'He loves me, he loves me not,

He loves me, he loves me not . . .'

Then she rose and staggered on until her foot stumbled against something hard: it was the hilt of Albrecht's fallen sword. With a mad

*It was all over
before anyone could move*

gleam in her eyes, she seized the hilt and pointed the blade towards her heart; as the onlookers recoiled in horror, she forced the sword-point between her breasts.

It was all over before anyone could move.

With red blood slowly staining her white dress, she danced falteringly round and round, fondly imagining she was dancing with her lover as of old. Her movements became weaker and weaker as her life-blood ebbed away. Alarmed at the icy coldness stealing over her, she stumbled along the fringe of frightened friends, as if seeking help. Finally, stopping at her mother, she fell senseless to the ground.

Giselle was dead.

As the royal party led Albrecht away, Berthe and the villagers were left to weep over the cold, still body of Giselle.

Somewhere deep in the forest stand tall pale trees whose gnarled roots, like so many thirsty snakes, bury themselves in the black and stagnant water of a pool. Water lilies spread their broad green leaves on the surface of the placid water which the moon silvers here and there with a trail of white spangles. Reeds with brown velvet plumes shiver and tremble in the cool night air; a bluish mist fills the gaps between the trees, giving them fantastic shapes.

The entire forest seems full of sighs and tears. Is it really the dew that has put a pearly tear on the tip of that blade of grass? Is it really the wind sobbing as it passes through the reeds?

No human foot has trod this way, yet why is the grass so flattened with the stamp of many feet?

At the foot of a willow, asleep and concealed beneath the grass and flowers, lay poor Giselle. From the marble cross at the head of her grave hung, quite fresh still, the garland of vine leaves with which she had been crowned Queen of the Grape Harvest.

It was into this eerie moonlit glade that there now appeared Myrtha, Queen of the Wilis, floating on gossamer wings. Her beautiful face and frail arms were deathly pale as she glided through the trees, summoning her sisters to rise up from their graves and follow her. At once the Wilis came, veiled and with their arms crossed over their breasts. On a command from the pale queen, they dropped away their veils and stood around Giselle's fresh grave.

Then, as the queen raised her green myrtle branch above the grave, the ghostly figure of the dead Giselle rose out of the earth, her eyes closed, her arms crossed over the wound in her heart. She walked slowly towards Myrtha who, in an instant, plucked off the dead girl's veil and laid an icy hand upon her breast.

As Giselle's lovely face was bared, she opened her eyes and, at the bidding of the queen, joined the other Wilis in a dance. Off they ran, tripping and whirling through the trees, dancing to their hearts' content.

Meanwhile, into the now-deserted glade came a lone figure bearing a lily wreath. It was Albrecht, heartbroken and full of remorse, searching for his loved one's woodland grave. Looking round he suddenly spotted the earthy resting place and hurried to place his lilies upon it. Then, in grief and despair, he sank to his knees, weeping without cease.

How long he stayed there he did not know; but suddenly he felt the gentle touch of a girl's hand upon his shoulder. Looking up with a start, he saw – could it be? Yes – his Giselle, more beautiful than ever, though deathly pale. As he went to take her in his arms, she seemed to leap into the

She seemed to leap
above him, just out of reach

air, hovering above him just out of reach. She allowed him to caress her satin shoes, to pass his hands lightly over her skirts, as if to reassure himself that she was real.

Yes, it was Giselle. But oh so cold. And so hard to catch. First she would be before him, talking of the happy days of their first love; then she was flitting through the trees while he ran, looking upward, trying to keep her in view.

In the meantime, another mortal man came running into the glade, looking fearfully behind him. It was Hilarion, also seeking the grave of his lost Giselle. But he, poor man, fell victim to the waiting Wilis, ever seeking a lone wayfarer in the forest to wreak their revenge on all mankind.

From out of nowhere, several Wilis appeared to bar his path. Whichever way he turned he could not evade their grasping hands. They passed him from hand to hand as they formed a giant ring about him. As he caught sight of the smiling queen, he made towards her, falling at her feet and begging her to spare him.

She coldly refused.

He retraced his steps, circling around, entreating each Wili in turn, but each one laughed in his face and pushed him on to her companion: round and round he went in a frenzied dance until he was weak and dizzy. Suddenly, the ring about him opened and, as he reached the end of the line, the last two Wilis pushed him down into the brackish pool. And he was drowned.

How the Wilis laughed with joy.

Having tasted blood, they were now even more eager to deal with the other victim they knew to be in their haunted glade. Mercilessly they sought out Albrecht and dragged him before Myrtha, their queen. On his knees he begged for mercy, but she had no pity in her heart, and commanded the Wilis to engage him in their frenzied dance.

How Giselle wished to save him.

She did what she could to shield him, urging him meanwhile to make for the safety of the marble cross above her grave. Despite the efforts of the Wilis, who had to shield their eyes from the radiance of the cross, Albrecht reached it and clung on grimly. Towering above Giselle and Albrecht, Myrtha, Queen of the Wilis, raised her magic branch once more to strike him down – but its magic was useless against the cross, and it snapped in her hand.

With the Wilis turning their heads away and covering their eyes with upraised arms, the queen, full of hate, again approached the grave and commanded Giselle to dance.

She had to obey her queen, and dance with Albrecht.

Yet she did so gently and lovingly. Several times he fell to his knees exhausted as the dance went on throughout the night. But each time Giselle helped him up. On and on went the unceasing dance until, finally, he sank down to the ground and rose no more.

But just as Myrtha and the Wilis thought they had triumphed, the first cold breath of dawn blew through the haunted glade. A distant cock announced the sunrise and church bells struck the hour of four.

At once the Wilis sank to their knees and slowly vanished into the mossy ground. Their power was over for another night, and Albrecht had survived through the strength of Giselle's love.

Giselle longed to remain with her beloved. But being a Wili, she had to return to her grave. Slowly and reluctantly she drifted from her lover's side and stood upon her grave. Desperately, Albrecht tried to prevent her going, but he could not fight the magic of the Wilis. With the rising of the sun above the trees, she faded from sight like the other spirits of the night, and Albrecht fell sobbing across her grave.

Dearly did he pay for faithless love.

Nutcracker

The stories of the German writer E.T.A. Hoffmann provided inspiration for many musical diversions, the best known being The Tales of Hoffmann *(Offenbach),* The Flying Dutchman *(Wagner),* Coppelia *(Delibes) and* Nutcracker *(Tchaikovsky). His long story* The Nutcracker and the Mouse King *inspired the French writer Alexandre Dumas to write a fairy story Casse-Noisette or Nutcracker; it was this that Peter Tchaikovsky used as the basis of his ballet.*

He composed the ballet a year after Sleeping Beauty *and a year before his death in 1893, and it was first performed on December 17, 1892 at the Marinsky Theatre in Saint Petersburg. The magnificent costumes and scenery were the creation of the great French-born choreographer Marius Petipa.*

Once again Tchaikovsky provided innovations that shocked the purists, creating a number of musical effects played on toy instruments: these included a rattle (to produce the sound of Nutcracker cracking nuts), a toy trumpet, a triangle, a snare drum and cuckoo and nightingale whistles.

He even sent his friend and publisher, Jurgenson, abroad to buy a celeste to reproduce the dainty steps of the Sugar Plum Fairy. No one in Russia had seen a celeste before and Tchaikovsky was so afraid Rimsky-Korsakov or Glazunov would use it first that he shrouded the whole operation in great secrecy before the performance.

The arrival
of the celeste

The tree bore apples
of silver and gold

NUTCRACKER

I T was Christmas Eve. Clara and Fritz Silberhaus were not allowed to enter the drawing room. Not at all. They had to sit in the back parlour all day long, waiting excitedly to see their presents.

Just after tea they had seen a little wrinkled man creep across the hallway with a big box underneath his arm. When she set eyes on him, Clara clapped her hands with joy. For it was their godfather, Mr Drosselmeier.

'I wonder what he has for us this time?' she whispered.

Mr Drosselmeier was a very clever man who could even mend clocks and watches. Whenever one of the household clocks went wrong, he would come, take off his yellow jacket, put on a blue apron and set to work. He would soon make the clock whirr and tick and chime as merrily as ever. Of course, each time he came he was sure to bring some gift in his pocket for the children. But for Christmas he always brought something special that he had made himself.

The children went on discussing what treats might be in store for them this time, until, at last, a tinkling bell sounded and the doors of the drawing room opened wide. Father and Mother appeared, took the children by the hand and led them in to see their presents.

The big Christmas tree in the corner bore apples of silver and gold; its branches were hung with sugared almonds, barley sugar, brightly-coloured sweets of every flavour and delicious bonbons. Right at the top was the lovely Sugar Plum Fairy.

Clara's eye was caught by a pretty silk dress with coloured ribbons hanging from a branch. In the meantime, Fritz had spotted a fine regiment of toy soldiers beneath the tree. They had sparkling red and gold uniforms and carried silver swords: They were mounted on such gleaming horses you would have thought they were of purest silver too.

While Fritz was mustering his hussars, Clara noticed a very handsome little man standing quietly by the tree, as if waiting patiently to be observed. His body was a mite too tall and heavy for his legs, and his head was much too large for his body. But his uniform was magnificent: he wore a scarlet hussar's jacket with gold braid upon the shoulders, trousers of Prussian blue and shiny black boots. Draped across his shoulders was a short blue cloak, and he had on his head a tall black officer's hat. He was quite splendid.

As Clara stared at this hussar, she saw the kindness in his face. Those green eyes of his beamed with goodness; and his well-kept cotton beard set off the smile upon his bright red lips.

'Oh, Daddy,' cried Clara, 'whose is that lovely little man beside the tree?'

'Well now,' said Father, 'that fellow will serve you all by cracking nuts. He is a nutcracker.'

Turning to Mr Drosselmeier, he asked him to demonstrate the toy he'd made.

Thereupon, Mr Drosselmeier picked up the little soldier and lifted the

end of his wooden cloak: at once the gallant soldier opened his mouth wide, displaying two rows of very white, sharp teeth. Mr Drosselmeier put a nut in the soldier's mouth and – crack – he had bitten the shell in two. Clara ate the nut.

'Since you have taken such a liking to him, Clara,' said Mr Drosselmeier, 'he shall be in your charge, if your Father does not mind.'

Clara instantly took the nutcracker in her arms and picked up more nuts for him to crack – but she chose the very smallest so that he would not hurt his teeth.

After a while, Fritz tired of playing with his soldiers and wanted to try out Nutcracker too. He gave him the biggest and hardest nuts he could find, and all at once three bottom teeth fell out of the Nutcracker's mouth and his jaw grew wobbly.

Clara snatched him from her brother, quickly wrapped the wounded soldier in her lace handkerchief and tied a pretty ribbon about his chin. Thus she held him gently, rocking him like a doll as she read her picture books.

It was getting late, not far off eleven. Godfather Drosselmeier had gone home long before. Most of the toys had been stored tidily in the glass cupboard, and it was now long past bedtime. Finally, the whole family went happily to bed.

But Clara could not sleep. She tossed and turned, unable to get poor Nutcracker from her mind. At last she decided to creep downstairs and put the wounded soldier in the doll's cot, so that he should not be frightened, alone in the strange dark house.

She threw back the bedclothes, got out of bed, opened her bedroom door as quietly as she could and crept downstairs. As she reached the bottom stair her heart leapt to her mouth as, suddenly, the grandfather clock in the hallway began to chime – one, two, three . . . right up to twelve.

It was Christmas Day.

She opened the drawing-room door very quietly, tiptoed to the cupboard and took down the poor pale Nutcracker from the shelf.

'My darling little soldier,' she softly said. 'I shall nurse you back to health again. Your teeth will soon be mended – Godfather Drosselmeier will see to that.'

Carefully, she removed her doll, Miss Marie, from the doll's cot and put the wounded soldier in her place. She wrapped another ribbon round his chin and drew the bedclothes up to his nose. Then she closed the cupboard doors and was going back to bed herself when she heard a sort of whispering noise.

As she listened it grew louder and seemed to come from all parts of the room – from behind the stove, under the chairs, out of the cupboards.

She stood rooted to the spot.

Almost at once she heard the sound of running, as if thousands of tiny feet were pattering behind the walls and underneath the floorboards. And thousands of tiny lights began to glimmer through the woodwork. No, they were not lights: now she could see that they were little gleaming eyes!

Everywhere hordes of mice were peeping and squeezing through every nook and cranny in the room.

Then a great hideous beast with seven heads and seven shining crowns appeared through the floorboards, hissing and squealing horribly. At once the mice formed ranks and regiments and, at an order from their king, advanced towards the cupboard.

Poor Clara, half fainting with fright, fell backwards and felt her elbow smash the glass of the cupboard door. At the sound of breaking glass, the Mouse King and his army stopped in their tracks and began to retreat in disarray. Above her head Clara caught the peal of bells and faint voices whispering from the cupboard:

'Come awake this night,
    To fight, to fight.
Sound the drums,
    The Mouse King comes.'

As Clara glanced up at the cupboard shelves, she saw that her dolls were in a panic, but Nutcracker had risen from his bed and was waving his little sword, shouting to everyone to follow him into battle.

At his call, all the lids of the boxes in which Fritz's hussars were quartered burst open and the toy soldiers lined up to fight. And together with the Nutcracker they all came leaping down from the shelves.

The mouse army had again massed, ready to charge, under the command of the terrible seven-headed Mouse King.

Before Clara's frightened gaze, the two armies clashed head on. The hussars and the mice were soon enjoined in desperate sword fights while Fritz's gunners pounded the mice with sugar plums and gingernuts. Clara

*Then a great hideous beast with seven
heads and seven shining crowns appeared,
hissing and squealing horribly*

could scarcely see the battleground for dust and smoke. But above the hurly-burly could be heard Nutcracker's brave voice issuing commands.

Then, in the thick of the battle, Clara saw two foes seize Nutcracker by his blue cloak and hold him fast while the Mouse King rushed towards him, squeaking in triumph from all his seven throats at once. Clara could contain herself no longer. Taking her slipper off, she threw it as hard as she could, straight at the hideous king.

Everything vanished in an instant. All was still.

Poor Clara, suddenly feeling the sharp pain in her arm, fell senseless to the floor.

When she awoke she was lying on her bed, the sun was pouring through the window and her mother was standing anxiously above her.

'Oh Mother,' said Clara weakly, sitting up in bed, 'are all those horrid mice gone? Is Nutcracker safe?'

'Don't bother your head with such nonsense,' said her mother. 'You've had us all quite worried. Thank heaven I awoke just after midnight and heard you moving about downstairs. I found you lying in a faint before the cupboard, your arm was bleeding and a pane of glass was broken.'

Mother was obviously put out.

'What were you doing?' she continued. 'There were lead soldiers scattered round you, pieces of gingerbread and sweets strewn about, your slipper was missing and there was Nutcracker lying on the floor close to your injured arm . . .'

Clara shook her head. She couldn't explain. 'I think I was dreaming,' she said.

'Too much excitement,' said her mother. 'Now just you get some rest and go back to sleep.'

As Mother left the bedroom, Clara's head sunk once more upon the pillow. She shut her eyes and went to sleep.

How long she slept she did not know, but all of a sudden she awoke with a start, roused by a gentle tapping at the door and a soft voice calling, 'Clara, Clara, open the door.'

Who could it be?

She did not recognise the voice at all.

Putting on her dressing gown she ran across the room and opened the door. There stood Nutcracker. But he was not a stiff wooden soldier any more; now he was a handsome young man.

He knelt down on one knee and said, 'It was you, dearest lady, who saved my life and, in so doing, broke the spell which the Mouse King had put upon me. No longer am I a nutcracker. I am myself once more: a proud prince, free to return to my own kingdom in Bonbon Land. Would you like to come with me?'

Clara was still a little dazed, too surprised to utter a word. At last she said, 'Yes, I'd love to go with you, dear Prince. But it must not be far because I must be back for dinner.'

'Then we shall go by the shortest route,' Nutcracker said, throwing his cloak about her.

Clara felt herself floating through the air and out of the room, timidly holding the hand of the handsome prince. She glanced down as they were flying over her town and out across the forest, gliding in and out of snow-covered fir trees. Soon everything was blotted out by swirling snowflakes – though Clara did not feel cold at all.

Then Clara had another shock. As she looked closer, she saw that each snowflake was really a tiny fairy dressed in white, dancing in the sky. When

*The journey seemed
to take no time at all*

a very big snowflake whirled towards them, Clara knew at once by the crown and glittering white gown that this was the Snow Queen.

The prince bowed, Clara curtseyed, and they were both swept off in a swirling waltz by the Snow Queen, with thousands of snowflake fairies dancing in attendance. They flew between the snowcapped peaks, over white valleys and the rooftops of strange villages. Finally, at the Queen's command, some of the fairies gathered together to form an ice-blue sleigh that took the prince and Clara down a frozen river to Bonbon Land.

The journey seemed to take no time at all, for Clara had hardly blinked before she found herself climbing out of the sleigh on to a sunny shore. She was standing in a sweet-scented meadow surrounded by tiny star-like flowers.

'This is Candy Meadow,' explained Prince Nutcracker. 'Let us go through the gate over there that leads to the palace.'

Clara looked up and saw a beautiful gateway at the far end of the meadow. It seemed to be made of white and brown marble; yet as she approached she saw it was really made of nougat, raisins and sugared almonds. Above the gateway was a gallery made of barley sugar.

Presently, the sweetest of smells came to her from a little wood on both

sides of the path. On the dark green firs Clara could see gold and silver fruits hanging from the boughs. An orange perfume wafted to her as if on zephyr wings, and a breath of wind made all the leaves and branches rustle and tinkle as at Christmastide.

'How charming it all is,' cried Clara, clapping her hands with joy. 'What is this wood?'

'It is Christmas Wood,' replied the prince.

They continued along the marble path which Clara could now see was made of many sorts of sweets. They were walking by the side of a gently rippling brook from which came the orange perfume that filled the air.

'This is Orange Brook,' said Prince Nutcracker. 'Its fragrance is nowhere near as fine as that of Lemonade River which travels far and cascades into the Sea of Almond Milk.'

Indeed, Clara soon heard a loud splashing and rushing as she came in sight of Lemonade River, which went rolling along in swelling amber waves between banks of lollipop trees and sherbert ferns.

They were now in sight of a dazzling palace. This time Clara was not at all surprised to see that it was made of icing sugar with marzipan domes.

Once inside, she was led into a grand ballroom with a marshmallow ceiling supported by twisting barley-sugar pillars. Its butterscotch walls were decorated with rich bouquets of sugar violets, tulips, carnations and lilies of the valley; their glowing colours enhanced the rosy pink of the walls.

As Clara stepped, enchanted, across the pink and white mosaic of

Turkish Delight covering the floor, she was offered a golden chair with a satin cushion.

Prince Nutcracker clapped his hands, and at once there appeared a party of little shepherds and hunters, so white and delicate you would think they were made of icing sugar. Before Clara in her golden chair, the shepherd boys and girls performed a pretty ballet, to which the hunters played music on their horns.

Then, in turn, came a Spanish Chocolate Dance, an Arabian Mocca Coffee Dance, a Chinese Tea Dance, and a Russian Trepak Dance. Clara especially liked the Trepak which got faster and faster until her head swam with the music and the flying feet.

But best of all she liked the dance of the Sugar Plum Fairy. How beautiful the Fairy was in her rose-coloured gown, gliding about the ballroom to the tinkling music of tiny bells.

When her dance was over, she invited all the guests to join in a final waltz, and Clara's heart beat fast when the handsome prince asked her to dance. As they whirled around the ballroom, sweet-scented petals and orange blossom floated down gently from the ceiling.

Clara was so happy dancing to this waltz of flowers in the prince's arms that she no longer heard the music; it seemed to fade into the distance and a silver mist rose up around her in which she and the prince, the Sugar Plum Fairy, and all the other dancers were floating. She seemed to be rising up, up, up, as if carried on scudding clouds.

Then came a hard bump and a tumble.

Clara opened her eyes and . . . she was lying on the bedroom floor in a heap of bedclothes; the broad light of Christmas Day was streaming through the window. From downstairs she could hear her mother's voice, calling her to dinner.

'Clara, Clara, wake up. Dinner's ready.' There was a pause and then her mother continued, 'Come along, my dear.'

Clara rubbed her eyes.

'I know,' she said, 'I must have fallen asleep in Nutcracker's arms, and he has brought me home and put me back in bed.'

She told no one of her adventures: the sparkling Christmas Wood, the beautiful Snow Queen, the dazzling palace of icing sugar with its marzipan domes, the Sugar Plum Fairy and the handsome prince. It was a secret she shared with Nutcracker. In any case, such wonders can be seen only by those with eyes to see them.

The Stone Flower

The story is based on folk tales collected by Pavel Bazhov, who learned the unwritten history of the Urals Mountains while working as a boy in the old malachite mines. His tale Kamenny tsvetok (The Stone Flower) was included in his collection Malakhitovaya shkatulka (The Malachite Box), published in Sverdlovsk in 1939.

Sergei Prokofiev wrote the music and Mikhail Lavrovsky provided the choreography. The ballet was first produced at Moscow's Bolshoi Theatre on February 12, 1954, with a 'star–studded' cast including Galina Ulanova, Maya Plisetskaya, Vladimir Preobrazhensky and Alexei Yermolaev. Despite this, it was not a success. It was not until three years later, when Grigorievich choreographed a new production for Leningrad's Kirov Theatre (the old Marinsky) on April 27, 1957 that the new ballet was acclaimed in what has now become its standard version.

The Kirov Theatre in the 19th century

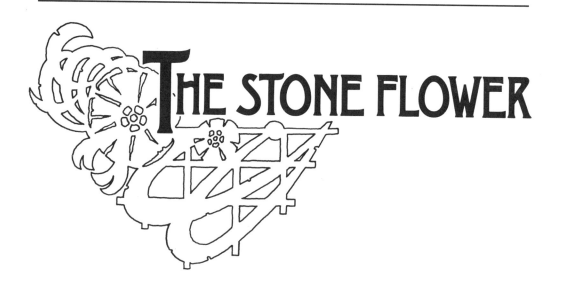

THE STONE FLOWER

THERE was a craftsman in the old days called Prokopich – the best malachite carver in the Urals, so folk said. When he was getting old the Master decided to give him an apprentice. But old Prokopich – perhaps because he did not want to give away the secrets of his craft, or perhaps because he was just plain stubborn – did not teach any lad much. All they got from him were cuffs and blows. He would all but pull their ears off, then tell the Master, 'They're no good. Their eyes aren't straight and they've two left feet instead of hands. They'll never learn.'

Finally it was Danilo the orphan's turn.

He was twelve or a little more. A tall, spindly lad, thin as a rail, yet with a pleasing face, blue eyes and fair curly hair. To begin with he'd been a page boy up at the manor house; but he'd stand around dreaming, staring at pictures or decorations, and never answering when his name was called.

At first they beat him, but soon gave up. 'Head in the clouds. Not smart enough. Never make a servant.'

So the Master sent him to old Prokopich; and the crusty old craftsman would have sent the lad packing too had he not caught him looking closely at a slab of malachite on the workbench one day.

'Seems to me, Grandad, you're cutting it wrong. Look, here's where the pattern goes,' Danilo said.

The boy traced the dark green lines with his finger as Prokopich began to shout and curse.

'Who do you think you are? A master craftsman? Seen now't, know now't and telling me my job! What do you know about it?'

'I know you're spoiling it, that's all,' Danilo said.

'Seems to me, Grandad,
you're cutting it wrong'

The old man went on raving at Danilo, but he did not pull his ear or cuff his head. In fact, he'd puzzled a good while over the stone himself, as to where to cut the border. Danilo was quite right. So Prokopich shouted himself hoarse, then said grudgingly, 'All right, if you're so clever, show me how it should be done.'

Danilo pointed here and there, 'Look, the pattern goes this way, so you could cut round it here and not disturb its beauty.'

Prokopich growled, 'Hm . . . aye . . . you're full of good ideas. If tongues were hands, they'd make light work.'

But he mused to himself: 'the lad's right. Something ought to come of this one.'

Now, Prokopich had never had a family of his own, and for some reason Danilo the orphan just caught at his heart. That night when the lad was asleep, he fetched his sheepskin coat to cover Danilo's skinny frame. The boy slept on, breathing heavily with just a trace of whistle. Prokopich wondered how he could make him sturdier.

'A sickly lad like that to learn my trade! The dust – it's poison, it'll get into his chest in no time at all. I'll put some flesh on his bones first, then teach him the trade. There's a craftsman in him all right.'

As the months went by Danilo grew stronger under the old man's care and they grew fond of one another: like father and son. Prokopich gave him

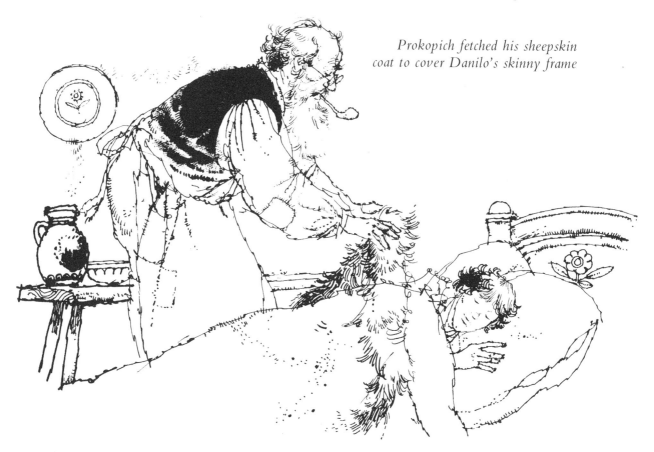

Prokopich fetched his sheepskin coat to cover Danilo's skinny frame

some work: simple things at first – brooches and snuff-boxes. Then it was carved candlesticks, till at last it came to really fine carving: petals and leaves, flowers and trees. It's a hard craft, working with malachite: the result may not look much, but the hours it takes to achieve it! Well, Danilo grew up on it.

The Master was so pleased with his handiwork that one day he sent a special order with a sketch for Danilo to copy. It was for a malachite vase to stand in the hall of the manor house. The vase was to have a bouquet of leaves at the top, two delicate handles at the side, and a base like that of the tsar's throne.

Danilo made the vase. It took him three long years, and when it was finally finished he and Prokopich invited all the craftsmen from miles around to come and celebrate, as was the custom in those parts.

Danilo sat listening to the words of praise: 'Line for line with the sketch. Not a single flaw. Couldn't be bettered. And done in double time too. If you go on like this we'll have a job to match you.'

Danilo shook his head. 'That's just the trouble with it. Clean and smooth, the pattern as plain as the sketch. But where's the beauty in it? Now take a flower, say a common daisy: when you look at it, it brings joy to your heart. It's so alive. Yet my vase is dead. The gentry will look and say: 'What an eye, what a hand. That fellow who made it; where did he get the patience to carve and not break the stone?' Yet it can never equal nature.'

The craftsman all told Danilo the same as Prokopich always said, 'Stone's stone. Our job's to cut and grind, polish and toil, nothing more.'

But there was an old, old man sitting amongst them. He'd taught Prokopich in his time, and the others too. Though his eye was now dim and his hand shaky, he alone understood what the talk was about.

'You'd best keep off those thoughts, son, or you'll end up a mountain craftsman.'

'What do you mean?' asked Danilo. 'Who are the mountain craftsmen, Grandad?'

'They're workmen who live inside the mountain, but you never see them. They work for the Mistress of Copper Mountain. I saw some of their work once. Aye, now that's real craft for you. You've never seen the like. It was a stone snake, like you make for bracelets. Nothing like the ones here, I tell you. Our snakes are stone, but this was as if alive: a black line down its back, and eyes – you'd think it would spring up and bite you. They can do anything with stone. You see, they've set eyes on the Stone Flower, so they've a great gift for beauty and perfection.'

The guests went their ways, but the talk about the Stone Flower stayed with Danilo. He pestered old Prokopich with his questions.

'I couldn't tell you, son. I've heard tell of such a flower, but it's not for your eyes. If a man sees it, life loses all sweetness for him.'

His curiosity aroused, Danilo spent much of his time after that on Serpent Hill. The old copper mine had been empty for some time, all dug away; now all the layers were exposed with pieces of malachite rock there for the taking. One day, as Danilo was searching around, he found a big piece, shaped and patterned like a bush, its veins running upwards to the top. Just what he wanted.

Once home he set to work; day and night were one to him. First he trimmed away at the bottom and a beautiful vase began to take shape – even Prokopich said it made him want to touch it. Danilo carved the stem and slender leaves, then the cup – how it held together was a marvel. Yet somehow when he reached the top he was discontented. He'd lost the beauty. He could not sleep. He sat over his vase wondering how he could put it right.

Other craftsmen came to look – what more did he want? No one had ever made a vase like that before, yet still Danilo was unhappy.

'Very well,' he sighed at last, 'that's enough. It seems I can do no better. I cannot grasp the power of beauty.'

He made up his mind to leave his craft for a time and get married. He had long been courting Katya, his childhood love, but had put off marrying until the vase was finished. Now he hurried on the wedding and the day was fixed. Yet talk of the Stone Flower kept coming to his mind, and something seemed to draw him to Serpent Hill. So off he went in early autumn, on the eve of his wedding day.

Already the ground was sprinkled with frost and powdery snow. He went to the cut where he had found the stone, and came upon a cave. Thinking to shelter a bit from the wind, he went inside and sat down on a rock by the far wall. And he set to thinking once again of that Stone Flower. If only he could catch a glimpse of it.

All of a sudden, he felt a warm breeze caress his face, as if it was summertime. He lifted his head and there, opposite, sat the figure of a woman, faint and shadowy at first like greenish mist. Gradually she took firm shape. It was the Mistress of Copper Mountain; he recognised her at once by her green malachite robe and dazzling beauty.

It was the Mistress of Copper Mountain

'Well, Danilo,' she softly said, 'so nothing came of your vase? Don't lose heart. Try again. You shall have the stone you want.'

'No,' he replied. 'I can do no more. I wish to see your Stone Flower – I've heard so much about it.'

'That's easy enough,' she said, 'but you'll be sorry ever more.'

'You won't let me leave the mountain?'

'Why not? The way is open. But no one ever abandons me.'

Danilo begged to see the flower yet still she tried to put him off. She spoke of his bride-to-be and old Prokopich and how they would miss him.

'Life's not worth living unless I see the Stone Flower,' he replied.

'As you wish then,' she murmured, shaking her head. 'Come, take my hand and see my garden.'

The wall behind her parted and he found himself amidst tall trees made of stone – marble, serpentine, lapis lazuli, emerald and malachite. And yet they were like living trees, with little twigs, buds and leaves.

As the breeze made them sway, there was a tinkling like tiny bells. Underfoot the grass was made of stones too – of rubies, mica and emeralds. Although Danilo could see no sun, it was as bright as on a summer's day, light shining from golden serpents swaying and twisting through the trees and bushes.

The Mistress led him to a clearing where the ground was like brown soil, with jet black bushes all around. Green bells of malachite hung from the trees, and in each was a star of golden antimony. Glowing bees hovered over flowers of stone and the golden stars tinkled a lilting tune.

Right in the centre of the glade was the most beautiful sight of all: the Stone Flower – olive green, so delicately made it seemed to tremble and glow, breathe and sway in the golden light.

'Well, Danilo, you have seen my garden,' the Mistress said. 'Now you must go.'

She waved her hand and Danilo found himself sitting once more inside the cave. The wind howled miserably outside, the way it always does in autumn.

When Danilo got home he found guests waiting with his bride-to-be. At first he did his best to be polite: he played his flute, sang and danced; but as time went on he seemed to sink beneath a black cloud. When the party broke up he took Katya to her door and left without a word.

By the time he reached home, Prokopich was asleep. Danilo quietly lit the lamp, dragged his vase to the middle of the floor and sat gazing at it. The old man's coughing kept interrupting his thoughts. Prokopich was getting old and frail. That cough of his was like a knife in Danilo's heart; it reminded him of all their years together.

Suddenly the lad made up his mind. Taking a hammer, he brought it down on the vase so hard it broke into tiny pieces. That done, he ran from the house and disappeared. . . .

Some said he had taken leave of his senses and died somewhere in the forest – no doubt the wolves had got him. Others knew better: they said he had gone forever to the workshops of the Mistress of Copper Mountain. They were right and they were wrong.

After Danilo disappeared, Katya, his bride-to-be, remained unwed. Two years passed by, or maybe three, and she was getting past the age for marriage. In those parts, girls are reckoned old maids after twenty; lads seldom send matchmakers to such, it's mainly widowers who think of them. But Katya must have been a real beauty, for the lads kept calling. She would have none of them.

'I'm promised to Danilo,' she would say. 'I'm sure he will come back.'

She had heard Danilo talk of seeking malachite on Serpent Hill. So often that is where she went. One day, she climbed half way up the hill, and sat down on a rock. Every time she came there her heart ached as she remembered Danilo. And then, as now, when she was alone with nothing but the rock and trees around, she let the tears flow freely down her cheeks. Yet this was not like all the times before. For as she looked down she saw the ground open up beneath her feet, and a slope descend on to a sunlit plain.

Her heart beating wildly, she made her way down the slope and along the plain until she reached a forest. The trees were cold and smooth like polished stone; the grass beneath her feet was stony too. She walked on through the forest, calling out, 'Danilo-o-o. Where are you?'

Her call echoed through the woods, and the trees and bushes whispered back, 'Not here. Not here. Not here.'

But Katya would not give up her search. 'Danilo-o-o. Where are you?'

Stone twigs and branches swayed and hissed, 'Not here. Not here. Not here.'

Once more she cried, 'Danilo-o-o, where are you?'

Thereupon, the figure of a woman, like a wraith of green-grey mist, took shape before her, barring the way.

'Why do you come into my forest?' the Mistress of Copper Mountain asked. 'Is it stone you want? Take what you will and go.'

'No,' cried Katya, 'stone is dead. I want life. Give me back Danilo.'

The Mistress smiled and shook her head. 'Let him decide himself.'

All the while the forest had been dark, but now it was lit up: the grass sparkled with emerald dew, leaves glittered in a golden glow, stone flowers gleamed green and red and blue. It was all so beautiful you could feast your eyes and never tire.

'Danilo, where are you?'

But Katya's gaze was fixed on something else; for her dear Danilo was coming through the trees.

She would have rushed to meet him had not the Mistress commanded, 'Wait! Danilo, Mountain Craftsman, you must make your choice: either remain here, forgetting all mortal people; or go with her and abandon what is mine.'

Danilo looked from the Mistress to Katya, then down to his feet. After a while he looked up and smiled, 'I cannot forget living people,' he said. 'And Katya is ever in my thoughts.'

The Mistress gave a wistful smile. 'Take your craftsman,' she said to Katya. 'And for your work, Danilo, I have a gift for you. You may retain all the knowledge you have learned from me; but, one thing only – you must forget this place completely.'

In an instant the glade and stone flowers were all gone. They were standing on a hillside in the soft rays of dawn.

'Now return to your home,' the Mistress said. 'And mark well, Danilo: say no word about my mountain; tell folk you went away to a master craftsman in far-off parts to learn his skill. And you, Katya, do not think I lured your sweetheart away; he came of his own free will, without my bidding.'

'Forgive me,' Katya said, curtseying low.

'So be it. What can hurt stone?' the Mistress said, yet she seemed to sigh so deeply, it was like wind moaning in the trees. Then she faded clean away.

Danilo and Katya made their way quietly home without being seen. When the villagers passed Katya's cottage later that morning, they were surprised to see Danilo sitting by the window. At first they thought it was a ghost. But when they gathered round and saw him filling his pipe and puffing away contentedly . . . well, that settled it. Dead men do not smoke.

From then on Danilo and Katya lived together in their cottage. Folk say they were happy, never a cross word. Danilo was always called the Mountain Craftsman because of his fine work – none could rival him. So they lived well and had eight children. Only sometimes Danilo would grow dreamy and forgetful.

Katya knew what he was thinking, of course. But she always let him be.

Sleeping Beauty

The first story in Charles Perrault's Histoire ou Contes du temps passé, *published in 1697, was* La Belle au bois dormant – *The Beauty in the Sleeping Wood, or Sleeping Beauty as it is now known in English.*

It inspired Tchaikovsky to write a ballet that is judged by many to be the greatest ever written. The main addition by the composer to the original story comes at the end, where he inserted a quadrille featuring all the Perrault fairy tale characters: Little Red Riding Hood, Puss in Boots, Cinderella, Tom Thumb, Bluebeard and so on.

In the summer of 1889 Tchaikovsky frequently walked to a cottage in the depths of the forest to visit the four-year-old daughter of a forester. There he sang her songs and told her stories of beautiful princesses and magic castles in enchanted forests. That same winter when he had returned to Moscow he received news that she had died suddenly of diphtheria. He was heartbroken and he decided to write a ballet in her memory; putting all else aside, he worked for forty days and nights to compose a ballet of the little girl's favourite story – Sleeping Beauty.

The ballet had its premiere on January 15, 1890 in Saint Petersburg's Marinsky Theatre, with Carlotta Brianza dancing the part of Aurora. It was one of the most magnificent occasions in Russia's artistic history, with no expense spared.

When the curtain went up the audience, which included the Tsar and the Russian nobility, witnessed the most wonderful dancing, costumes and scenery they had ever seen. These were the creation of the French (later a naturalised Russian) choreographer Marius Petipa, set in the style of the French court of Louis XIV (hence King Florestan XIV in the story). As for the music, no one before or since has heard such grand music written for ballet.

The forester's little daughter

SLEEPING BEAUTY

THERE was once a King and Queen who were extremely distressed at having no children, they were more sad than words can tell. They took the waters at every spa, made countless vows and went on pilgrimages, in fact they tried all they could. Yet nothing helped.

And then at last, the Queen gave birth to a girl. How delighted was she and her husband King Florestan XIV. And how eager they were to share their joy.

A grand christening was held.

As godmothers to the little Princess, the royal pair invited all the fairies in the realm (there were six in all), since each would bring a gift – as was the custom with fairies in those days. So the Princess would have all the virtues imaginable: the greatest beauty in the world, the wisdom of an angel, grace and elegance, the voice of a nightingale, and talent to play any music she wished.

They called the baby Princess Aurora.

After the christening, the entire company returned to the palace for a banquet in honour of the fairies. And as each fairy arrived she was announced by a ringing fanfare and her name was called out by the Lord Chamberlain Cantalbrutte. Meanwhile, in one corner of the chamber the young Princess rested in her golden cradle watched over by her nursemaids.

As the first fairy arrived, Cantalbrutte's loud voice rang out, 'Your Royal Majesties: Candide, Fairy of the Crystal Fountain.'

She was dressed in the purest white. Curtseying low before the royal pair, she placed a gift – a garland of white water lilies – before the cradle.

*She placed a gift —
a garland of white lilies*

'Your Royal Majesties: Fleur de Farine, Fairy of the Meadow.' And a fairy entered wearing a flowing gown embroidered with wild flowers. Presenting a bouquet of cornflowers and poppies, daisies and celandine, she laid it gently beside the lilies.

Cantalbrutte's voice echoed round the hall once more. 'Your Royal Majesties: Violante, Fairy of the Woodland Glade.' This fairy was clad in the green of summer and the rust of autumn, and she knelt and placed a spray of cherry blossom before the sleeping child.

'Your Royal Majesties: Canarie, Fairy of the Song Birds.' Attired in dove grey and peacock blue; her gift was a canary in a golden cage.

'Your Royal Majesties: Mignonne, Fairy of the Golden Vine.' And she put before the cradle a basket of wild fruit; strawberry and grape, damson and bird cherry.

Then there was a pause and Cantalbrutte drew a long breath. After a while a last fanfare sounded. The assembled guests turned to see who was arriving now. A fairy of such beauty entered the hall and curtseyed low before the King and Queen. From her dress they could see that this was the Lilac Fairy. She lifted her wand above the sleeping child. As she did so, a violent clap of thunder echoed through the chamber, and a flash of lightning lit up the faces of the guests.

Aurora woke up at once and began to cry.

The doors of the chamber burst open, crashing back on their iron hinges, and in rushed a carriage drawn by four black-eyed grey rats; a pair of vultures circled menacingly overhead. It came to a halt before the royal cot and a witch-like creature in blood red robes stepped out. All around her was a mist of evil. It was the bad Fairy Carabosse.

No one had seen her for full fifty years and all had thought her dead or spirited away. So she had not been invited to the christening. Now, hissing curses between her teeth, she advanced upon the frightened child and, shaking a bony finger, set a curse upon the new-born babe.

'Before you are full grown, you shall die by pricking your finger on a spindle!' She cackled: 'You'll not forget me!'

This dreadful gift made the entire company tremble and begin to wail. Amidst the crying and the sobbing, the old Fairy Carabosse gave a last screech, stepped back in her carriage and rushed from the palace in a cloud of dust. Only then did the thunder cease.

There was a stunned silence save for the soft weeping of the guests, then came the Lilac Fairy's voice: 'Fear not, I have yet to make a gift. 'Tis true I

All around her was a mist of evil

can't undo what's said to come. But I can touch her with the thorn of sleep and she will slumber on for a hundred years – until a prince comes to wake her with a kiss.'

The people oohed and aahed and the King stepped forward to issue a proclamation:

> *'From this day forth, all spindles in the land*
> *must be destroyed – on pain of death!'*

The years passed by and Princess Aurora grew up to be the loveliest creature in the world; she had the wisdom of an angel; she was as graceful and stately as a silver birch; she danced divinely; when she lifted her voice to sing it was just like a nightingale; and her music on any instrument was as sweet as the summer wind through the tree-tops.

On her sixteenth birthday, a grand ball was held to celebrate and guests came from all over the kingdom and beyond: lord and lady, yeoman and squire, even four princes from over the sea – from Poland and Italy, from India and England. When the music played they each danced with her in turn and each presented her with a rose of his choosing.

In the midst of this festivity, as the Princess walked in the garden among her guests, she felt fingers clutch at her arm. And as she glanced round she was surprised to see an old dame in a dark red robe, leaning on a stick, her face hidden by a deep hood. The dame reached out her gnarled old hand and offered a bunch of bright red roses to the Princess.

'For your birthday, child. This is my present to you,' she said.

'Oh, how lovely,' exclaimed the flushed Princess.

Yet as she looked up to thank the woman, she was nowhere to be seen. No matter, the roses were so pretty and the Princess ran off to show her friends. As she reached her parents a sharp thorn pricked her finger and a spot of ruby blood appeared. As soon as she recalled the Fairy's warning, the colour drained from her face. But when nothing happened she knew the rose thorns could do no harm and her fear vanished. She began to pluck roses from the bouquet and offer them to her guests.

As she did so, however, she uncovered a tiny spindle concealed within the blooms and, in horror, flung it to the ground.

Alas, it was too late.

There was now no way of stopping the Fairy's spell and she fell down in a swoon.

The dame reached out her gnarled old hand. 'For your birthday, child,' she said

People crowded round: one sprinkled water on her face, another unlaced her bodice, others clapped her hands together, tickled her toes and rubbed her temples with rosewater. But nothing could bring her round. As the Queen looked about in despair she caught a fleeting glimpse of the red-robed figure standing beyond the crowd. Her hood had dropped from her head and she was laughing cruelly. At once the Queen recognised the evil face of Carabosse.

Realising that the prediction must now come true, King Florestan had his daughter carried to the finest chamber of his palace and laid upon a bed of gold and silver.

She was so beautiful that one might have taken her for an angel. Aurora's colour did not fade: her cheeks remained of red carnelion, her lips of brightest coral. And though her eyes were closed, people knew she was not dead by the gentle rise and fall of her breast.

She was indeed a Sleeping Beauty.

Far away in the land of Mataquin the Lilac Fairy was on her travels when

She was so beautiful that one might have taken her for an angel

the sad news of these events reached her ears. She left at once and, within an hour, arrived in her chariot drawn by four fiery dragons.

The King helped her down and led her sorrowfully to his daughter.

Of course, there was nothing she could do to disturb the Princess's sleep – not until the hundred years were up. But an idea came to her.

'The Princess will be lonely when she awakes, not seeing anyone she knows. I'll touch everything that lives and breathes with my magic wand and they will sleep as well.'

And so she did. Nursemaids, ladies of the bedchamber, courtiers, officers of the guard, stewards, cooks and pages, lackeys and footmen. Then she touched the horses in the stables, the dogs in the yard, even little Fido, the Princess's dog, lying beside her on the bed.

The instant she touched them they fell asleep. Even the spits on the fire, full of partridge and pheasant, began to slumber. The spell was cast in the time it takes for a butterfly to fold its wings.

The Lilac Fairy took her leave and there grew up around the palace a maze of tangled trees and brambles, thicket and thorn so twisted and laced together that neither man nor beast could pass that way at all. Nothing could be seen but the tops of the palace towers and only then from a long way off.

Sleeping Beauty was now safely protected from the idle gaze and curious talk of passers-by.

A hundred years passed on until, one day, a handsome Prince came hunting in those parts. His name was Prince Desiré, but because of his kind manner and friendly smile he was often called Prince Charming. Now, seeing the towers amidst the thick tangled wood, he asked each person he came across for news of the place. Each replied according to the tale he'd heard. Some said it was a ruined castle haunted by ghosts; others that all the warlocks for miles around held their sabbath there. Most thought an ogre dwelt within; he would carry off young children and eat them, bones and all, since no one could follow him through the wood.

The Prince was puzzled and didn't know what to think. But then an aged man spoke up, 'I once heard my father say some fifty years ago – he'd heard it from my grandfather – that the castle holds a beautiful Princess, that she must sleep a hundred years until awoken by a Prince's kiss.'

Excited by these words, the Prince wondered whether he was the man to disturb her dreams. Thereupon he resolved to break the spell cast upon her.

But when he approached the wood he gazed in dismay at the knotted mass of thorn and vine that blocked his way. How could anyone pass through? he thought.

He took a step towards the wood and, as he did so, the trees parted to let him through, and closed just as swiftly behind him to keep his attendants out – (the Lilac Fairy secretly watched, and as he walked, she cleared the way for him with her magic wand).

After a while he came to the castle courtyard where the sight that met his eyes would strike most men dumb: all around lay the bodies of people and animals. But when he peered more closely at the ruddy faces and ruby noses of the guards, he saw that they merely slept.

Crossing the marble courtyard he came to a flight of moss-covered steps that led steeply to the portals of what had once been a splendid palace. He climbed the steps, brushing aside the cobwebs and creepers hanging down, and passed more guards in ranks with dusty muskets upon their shoulders, all snoring loudly. He passed through several other chambers full of sleeping men and women, some standing, some sitting, others lying on the

floor. Everywhere the air was cool and damp, for no light could penetrate the vine-covered windows.

At last he came to a chamber with a single bed of gold and silver standing in the centre. There upon the bed was the most lovely girl he had ever seen. His heart grew tender and, trembling, he fell upon his knees beside her sleeping form. Softly he kissed her on the brow.

*'Is it you, my Prince?
I have waited so long'*

At once the spell was broken. The Princess awoke. She stared uncertainly at the stranger, then slowly her gaze softened to one of tender love.

'Is it you, my Prince?' she murmured. 'I have waited so long.'

They assured each other that their love was dearer than life itself; that they would ever be loyal and true. To tell the truth, he was more at a loss for words than she, and we need not wonder at it. After all, she had had time to think of what to say, for it is sure the Fairy had given her pleasant dreams during her long sleep. Though they talked together for hours on end, they could not find words enough to say what was in their hearts.

In the meantime, loud noises reached their ears as the palace began to awake. Limbs were stretched and a great bustling began as maids and men dashed about the halls and chambers on their chores. Muskets and swords clanked as the guards straightened up their shoulders and went about their duties. The King and Queen gave orders for supper – not being in the first fond flush of love they were now extremely hungry (not having eaten for a hundred years); the horses neighed, the dogs barked, and little Fido yapped.

The palace suddenly grew light as doors and windows were thrown open and sunlight streamed in to melt the cobwebs clean away. The tangled wood retreated, revealing green lawns and neat rosebeds with not a single weed in sight.

As the Prince helped the Princess to rise, he remarked to himself how charming she looked, yet dressed in a gown like that his grandmother used to wear. And when the violins and oboes played at supper the tunes were most old-fashioned to his ear. Indeed, it was a hundred years since last they played.

After supper, the young pair were led by the King and Queen to the palace chapel where they were married without delay. Then came the grandest celebrations the world has ever seen. The six Fairy godmothers were there, and so were all the favourite characters from fairyland; each had come to pay compliments to the happy couple.

The music started up and the company all joined in the merriest of dances.

Red Riding Hood danced with the Big Bad Wolf. Beauty danced with Beast. Goldilocks danced with all three bears at once. Bluebeard danced with his first wife. Puss in Boots danced with Simple Jack. Cinderella danced with her Prince. And, funniest of all, Tom Thumb danced with the Giant.

To say the least, a good time was had by all.

No one gave a thought to the wicked Fairy Carabosse. Some say she had been deafened by her own thunder and blinded by her own lightning.

It served her right.

The time came at last for Princess Aurora and Prince Charming to go on their honeymoon. Leading the way to a nearby stream, the Lilac Fairy took them to a waiting boat. When they were safely seated, she waved her magic wand and three giant butterflies appeared; with silken threads they towed the boat gently out on to the water and it glided smoothly out of sight.

As the assembled company all waved farewell, the Lilac Fairy smiled contentedly, for she knew that good had triumphed over evil in the end.

COMMENTARY TO WORDS AND MUSIC

The folk themes re-told in this book inspired three Russian and one French composer to write some of the most beautiful and exciting music the world has ever known. But more than that, each one of these artists made innovations that marked a new stage in the development of ballet.

PETER TCHAIKOVSKY was born on May 7, 1840 in the small Urals town of Votkinsk. His father Ilya was a well-to-do gentleman with ten servants and his own retinue of a hundred Cossacks; he was the most important personage in Votkinsk, where he worked as chief inspector of the government iron works.

Tchaikovsky grew up mainly at boarding school, studied law and entered the Saint Petersburg Ministry of Justice as a clerk at the age of nineteen. It was only when he was twenty-three that he decided to dedicate his life to music; and for the next twenty years he studied under the famous Russian brothers, Anton and Nikolai Rubinstein, at the Saint Petersburg and Moscow Conservatories.

His own music bridged the gap between the Russian 'nationalist' (Borodin, Mussorgsky, Rimsky-Korsakov) and 'traditionalist' schools. Though based on Western techniques, it was born of the Russian soil, of the melancholy song of the wind across the steppe, of the anguished cry of the Russian people, full of both deep despair and surging hope.

During his fifty-three years, Tchaikovsky achieved world fame as no Russian before or since, through his songs and symphonies, operas and ballets, concertos and serenades. Of the world's most popular composers, Tchaikovsky is probably the easiest to listen to and enjoy.

Ironically, when he presented his three ballets they were met with cool, puzzled silence. It is hard to understand today just what he did in revolutionising ballet. If *Swan Lake* is the essence of poety in ballet, *Sleeping Beauty* is the essence of grandeur, and *Nutcracker* the essence of rich fantasy. Never before had ballet-goers heard scores of such proportions devoted to ballet. Never before had such choreography and such dancing been known – the one complementing the other.

After Tchaikovsky's three works, ballet could never again sink down to its old humdrum and tinselly form. His ballets contained courtly music, fairy music, the music of youth and love. As music for dancing it is almost without rival, expressing, and often demanding in sound, precisely the movements of a dancer. The composer provided the dancers with a new standard of music to interpret, inspired great choreographers like Marius Petipa to produce fine artistic work, and lifted ballet to the level of great art.

IGOR STRAVINSKY was born on June 5, 1882 in the small Russian town of Oranienbaum on the Gulf of Finland, not far from the then Russian capital of Saint Petersburg. His father Fyodor was already Russia's foremost bass and performed operatic roles regularly at the Marinsky Theatre.

Igor therefore grew up in the company of some of the best Russian musicians, artists and writers. At the age of nine, he was already a competent concert pianist and, in his teens, he taught himself musical composition before studying under the composer Rimsky-Korsakov, whom he always regarded as his spiritual father.

He rose to world fame in his late twenties when he was invited by the Russian impressario Sergei Diaghilev to present three ballets during the Russian season in Paris. Diaghilev's famous Ballets Russes company performed *Firebird* in 1910, *Petrushka* in 1911 and *The Rite of Spring* in 1913. The decor and the music, as well as the stories on which the ballets were based, all reflected the same interest in Russian folklore and the same love of colourful rhythmic expression.

Nonetheless, the three works were so novel and disturbing that there was even a riot at the first performance of *The Rite of Spring*. Not only was the music often demanding, Stravinsky had introduced into his ballets such innovatory devices as songs and spoken texts explaining the musical actions – thus establishing the basis of modern ballet.

But he had done more than that. Under the direction of Diaghilev, he had worked within a team of great artists, which included the choreographer Mikhail Fokine, the artists Alexandre Benois and Alexander Golovin, and the dancer Vaslav Nijinsky. Together they produced truly exciting works of art.

From 1910, Stravinsky lived outside his native Russia, first in France and then, from 1939, in the United States of America, where he died at the age of ninety in 1971.

Stravinsky had, perhaps, one of the most penetrating minds ever applied to music, yet this analytical searching often produced the most 'primitive' and rhythmically exhilarating music of the twentieth century.

SERGEI PROKOFIEV was born on April 23, 1891 in the village of Sontsovka in the Ukraine, the south western part of the Russian empire. His father was the manager of the Sontsov estates, so the family was well off. His mother played the piano and taught her son, soon discovering that he was extremely talented. By the age of ten he had his first professional contact, had written an opera, *Giant*, and played before large audiences.

In 1904, at the age of thirteen he enrolled in the Saint Petersburg Conservatory, where the famous composers Rimsky-Korsakov and Lyadov were professors; but he thought them dull and, in his words, 'got much more' from his older fellow-student and lifelong friend Nikolai Myaskovsky. As a birthday treat, his mother sent him to London at the end of his Conservatory course, where he saw the Sergei Diaghilev Ballets Russes, which impressed him greatly. This marked the start of a long association with Diaghilev and the Ballet Russes, and especially with Stravinsky who influenced him considerably in the early years.

Diaghilev, in fact, produced Prokofiev's ballet, *The Buffoon*, in Paris in 1921, by which time the composer was already living abroad, outside his native Russia. He first went to America in 1918 and stayed for nineteen months. There he produced his most famous opera *The Love of Three Oranges* (1919). Then, in 1920, he moved to Paris where he lived for the next eighteen years. He married the singer Carolina Codina in 1923, but later on, in his homeland, he married his second wife, Mira Mendelson, who helped him stage his ballets, *Cinderella* and *The Stone Flower*.

He returned home for good in 1938 and never went abroad again. He said he pined for 'the sound of Russian in my ears; I have to speak to people of my own flesh and blood for them to give me what I lack here abroad: their songs, my songs.'

By then he was already a famous composer, one of the most prolific that has ever lived. Altogether he wrote nine operas, eight ballets, seven symphonies as well as works for chorus, orchestra, soloists, piano, 'cello and violin, and music for stage and film.

He is best known for his *Classical Symphony*, written during the First World War, his ballet *Romeo and Juliet* (1936) and his symphonic poem *Peter and the Wolf*, intended to introduce children to the instruments of the orchestra. He worked on *Cinderella* during the Second World War, including in it the popular march from *The Love of Three Oranges*, and he produced it as a musical celebration for the Soviet people who had survived the terrible war against Nazi Germany.

The Stone Flower was his last ballet and was written in 1950, just three years before his death. He died on March 5, 1953, a month short of his sixty-second birthday.

ADOLPHE ADAM was born in Paris on July 24, 1803. His mother was the daughter of a distinguished doctor, while his father was a Professor at the Paris Conservatoire. So Adolphe grew up in a musical family. Not only was his father an accomplished concert pianist, he also wrote music, including seven sonatas for the piano, and standard piano textbooks for French schools.

As a boy Adolphe was very fond of music, but disliked study and practice; he much preferred improvising tunes of his own. Tired of his refusal to work hard, his mother finally sent him to boarding school where he had to take lessons in music. He made good progress and, at the age of seventeen, decided to make music his career. From 1821 he studied at the Conservatoire, yet tended to concentrate on composing light music for operettas and the music hall.

In November 1847 he founded the National Opera devoted to the work of young composers. But the revolution of the following year meant the theatre's closure and financial disaster for Adam. By working immensely hard, however, he managed to pay off his debts by 1852, yet the overwork undermined his health and he died four years later on May 3, 1856 at the age of fifty-three.

Although Adam has gone out of fashion, apart from the music for *Giselle*, he wrote an extraordinary amount of music in his brief life span. Altogether, he wrote forty comic operas and fourteen ballets as well as masses, cantatas, choruses and songs. As a composer he worked swiftly and tirelessly, with a craving to write and create. He did much of his writing at night: as he put it, 'It is so pleasant to write in the evening; you have the entire night before you. In the daytime, there are so many disturbances.'

He composed the music for *Giselle* in 1841 in just eight days. It is not great music, unlike much of the music of Tchaikovsky, Prokofiev and Stravinsky; but it abounds with flowing melodies and simple dance rhythms. And since ballet is a composite art, it is not entirely fair to consider the music apart from the dancing – only in actual performance of a ballet can the worth of its musical score be assessed fully and fairly. As a ballet, *Giselle* has certainly stood the test of time and ranks today as one of the most popular ballets in the world.

SOURCES

In interpreting these seven stories I have attempted to steer a course between the original tales and the musical scores, thereby remaining as true as possible to the original sources, while enabling ballet-lovers to follow the plots of the musical performances.

In the case of *Sleeping Beauty*, I have consulted Charles Perrault's *La Belle au bois dormant* and adapted it to the Russian libretto of Marius Petipa and Ivan Vsevolozhsky, used by Tchaikovsky (I consulted this manuscript in the Tchaikovsky museum at Klin, near Moscow). The French source is *Perrault, Contes Edition de Jean-Pierre Collinet*, published by Gallimard, Paris, 1981.

Nutcracker is from E.T.A. Hoffmann's *Der Nussknacker und der Mauskönig*, although Petipa's Russian outline for Tchaikovsky is but a pale shadow of the original. I have also consulted Dumas's *Casse-Noisette* on which Tchaikovsky's ballet was mainly based.

I have not found a German original for *Swan Lake* (perhaps one does not exist?), although there are plenty of 'wandering' folk tales based on the swan-maiden theme. See, for example, the German *Schwannensee* and the French *Chevalier au cygne* cycles. In a letter to his friend, a German duke, Tchaikovsky says with some irony '. . . let people think it a fairy story if they wish', indicating that he saw the story representing his own tortured personality. I have, in fact, followed the Russian libretto written by V.P. Begichev and V.F. Geltser, with one exception: I have rejected the original fatalistic ending (where Odette and Prince Siegfried both drown) for the optimistic ending used in later Russian productions of the ballet.

For *Petrushka* there exists no recorded Russian folk tale; in this case I have based the story on the ballet's libretto by Stravinsky and Benois, and on the Russian puppet theme.

Cinderella straightforwardly comes from Perrault's *Cendrillon*, although once again I have consulted the Russian libretto of *Zolushka*.

With *Giselle* I have dipped into Heinrich Heine's wonderful poetry on which the original idea was based, and then stuck fairly loyally to the equally poetic libretto of the French poet Théophile Gautier. The exception here is that I have changed the ending to fit in with the more common later versions of the ballet.

The Stone Flower has a fond place in my memory. On my first visit to Russia back in 1959, I went to Sverdlovsk in the Urals and fell victim to Russian hospitality; – while recovering, a wonderful old Russian woman, Anastasia Booshueva, sat by my hotel bedside telling me the exciting stories of the Urals folk-tale collector Pyotr Bazhov. And the first of those was *The Stone Flower*. It was not the best cure for vodka, but it did inspire me to translate it into English many years later.

JAMES RIORDAN